KU-622-468

EAT SHOP SAV£

8 Weeks to Better Health

DALE PINNOCK

Hamlyn

An Hachette UK Company
www.hachette.co.uk

First published in Great Britain in 2019 by Hamlyn,
a division of Octopus Publishing Group Ltd
Carmelite House
50 Victoria Embankment
London EC4Y 0DZ
www.octopusbooks.co.uk

Text copyright © Dale Pinnock 2019
Design and layout copyright © Octopus Publishing Group Limited 2019
Photography copyright © Faith Mason 2019
Television series *Eat Shop Save* copyright © ITV Studios Limited 2017

All rights reserved. No part of this work may be reproduced or utilized
in any form or by any means, electronic or mechanical, including
photocopying, recording or by any information storage and retrieval system,
without the prior written permission of the publisher.

The right of Dale Pinnock to be identified as the author of this work has been
asserted by him in accordance with the Copyright, Designs and Patents Act 1988.

ISBN 9780600636328

A CIP catalogue record for this book is available from the British Library.

Printed and bound in China

10 9 8 7 6 5 4 3 2 1

Editorial Director: Eleanor Maxfield
Senior Editor: Sophie Elletson
Design and Art Direction: Smith & Gilmour
Photography: Faith Mason
Food Styling: Phil Mundy
Props Stylist: Olivia Wardle
Production Manager: Caroline Alberti

CONTENTS

INTRODUCTION 06

CHAPTER 1
SOUPS & SMOOTHIES 12

CHAPTER 2
SALADS 30

CHAPTER 3
MEAT 56

CHAPTER 4
FISH & SEAFOOD 84

CHAPTER 5
PLANT BASED 112

CHAPTER 6
BOWL FOOD 140

CHAPTER 7
SWEET TREATS 164

MEAL PLANNERS 188

INDEX 204

INTRODUCTION

Eat Shop Save: 8 Weeks to Better Health is here to prove to you once and for all that eating healthily can be simple, affordable and enjoyable – and benefit your life immeasurably. In the last book we gave you the basics to eat better, plan meals better, shop smart and save money. This book ticks all of the boxes as before – simple affordable recipes that the whole family can enjoy – but we're upping the health message.

Understanding good nutrition really IS your family's long-term health insurance. There is little else that will set the foundations for a long and healthy life than good nutrition. If you can take this information and actually make the food that you eat delicious, affordable and practical, well, then the magic happens.

The 8-week plan in this book will help you transition to healthier eating habits. It will show you what to build your diet around and get you on your way to eating wholesome, good-quality food. It will show you how to prepare healthy meals for all types of situations and, importantly, how easy, delicious and affordable it can be. This way of eating really is to help you have more years in your life and more life in your years. It's not about dropping a stone in thirty minutes, or getting a six pack overnight. It's about keeping you happy, healthy, energetic and vibrant, to enhance all aspects of your life. Believe me, life tastes much sweeter when you feel your best.

THE FOUNDATIONS OF A HEALTHY DIET

We visited some of these principles in the first book, but now we want to help get you into the swing of healthier habits for life. Build your diet with these principles in mind, and you are doing the best anyone can with the knowledge we have.

Nutrition is a science very much in its infancy. There is no escaping the fact that there is a great deal of conflicting information out there surrounding diet and health. Contradictory headlines. Divided opinions. It gets pretty crazy and most people are utterly confused. That being said, we do know a lot about the way in which our modern diet is destroying our health, so the most sensible option until we know better is to take this information and do the opposite. Here are some principles to build your diet around, and the results speak for themselves.

GET CARB SMART

Carbs are one of the hottest topics in the nutrition world right now and so many people habitually avoid them like the plague. This isn't necessary, but the carbs that many of us are eating are incredibly damaging to our health. The first thing to do? Ditch the white bread, white rice, white pasta, etc. From now on the white refined carbohydrates are out and the wholegrain varieties are in. Refined carbohydrates raise our blood sugar far too high far too quickly. In the

short term this can zap our energy levels. More seriously, however, is that in the long term it can raise cholesterol, increase weight gain that just won't shift, and dramatically increase your risk of type 2 diabetes. And the second thing to do is, once you swap over to brown bread, brown rice, wholewheat pasta, etc, cut your portion sizes in HALF!

By doing these two things you help keep blood sugar stable and within healthy parameters, which not only keeps your day-to-day energy on an even keel, but helps reduce those negative consequences of long-term blood sugar imbalance.

And another thing: wholegrain foods have the added benefit of being higher in fibre, which keeps you fuller for longer, thereby curbing cravings and preventing overeating. They are higher in important nutrients too.

BE CONSCIOUS OF FATS

Now, you may be surprised to see that the recipes in this book are not always low fat. Do not fear fat. For generations we have been led to believe that saturated fats are linked to heart disease and all fats cause us to...get fat. Boy was THIS information wrong. But it influenced public health messages and campaigns. We were told to completely avoid saturated fats and opt for 'heart healthy' vegetable oils instead, such as sunflower oil and those in margarine. This just made matters worse. Our diet ended up being too high in omega-6 fatty acids, which are fat-derived nutrients that are vital to our health, but in the correct ratio to omega-3 fatty acids. The amount of omega 6 that the UK population started consuming when we opted for the types of oils mentioned above, meant that these 'healthier' fats actually ended up contributing to MORE disease. This is because too much omega 6 can cause long-term inflammation in tissues, and this raises the risk of diseases such as – ironically – cardiovascular disease.

'So, what do I need to do about it?' I hear you say. Well, it is pretty simple: when it comes to cooking, use olive oil, because this contains hardly any omega-6 fatty acids. It is in fact composed mostly of omega-9 fatty acids, which are beneficial for heart health. Coconut oil is also a good choice. If you have sunflower oil, soy oil, vegetable oil, margarine etc, then throw them in the bin and never buy them again.

So, a final word about saturated fats: we were wrong to avoid them. The evidence is now clear that the link between saturated fat and heart disease isn't as obvious as it had previously been made out to be. Removing saturated fat from our diet led to two major changes to our diet that together had a hugely negative impact on our health. We started eating way more starchy foods than ever before, and started consuming more of those omega-6 fatty acids. These two factors together paved the way for a public health disaster – an increased risk of the modern degenerative diseases that plague our healthcare system today.

GET YOUR PLATE STRAIGHT

This step is super easy. It's what your plate should look like at each meal. You already know the portion of concentrated carbohydrates is going to be smaller than you may be used to. But don't worry, you're not going to go hungry. Your plate should also contain of a portion of good-quality protein and then the rest of the plate should be bulked out with non-starchy vegetables. Starchy vegetables include sweet potatoes, potatoes, parsnips, swede, etc. These will fall into your carbohydrate category. Generally, non-starchy veggies are anything else and, providing they're not swimming in a nasty sauce, you have a hall pass to eat as many of them as you like.

GET COLOURFUL

One of the main focal points of a healthy diet is colour variety. I want you to try to get as many different coloured plant foods into your diet as you possibly can. Each colour represents different groups of phytochemicals (chemicals in plants that can have beneficial effects upon our health), and as you go through the book you will see that many of the Nutrition Nuggets discuss certain foods and the phytochemicals that are in them that give them their colour and benefit our health. Variety is key. The more the merrier.

GET FRESH

The final thing is simply to remember this: every single meal is an opportunity to get some fresh stuff in. It doesn't have to be perfect, just find a way. Of course the ideal scenario would be to get you cooking from the book every day, but we do live on planet Earth, so we are realistic. Adding fresh foods into your day could be as simple as some berries on your morning porridge or a side of spinach with your cooked breakfast. It could mean snacking on fresh fruit or vegetable crudités between meals. Perhaps making sure you have a hearty side salad (no manky old lettuce) with your lunch, or two to three types of vegetables with your dinner. Sadly we are in an age of convenience foods. This means foods that have been heavily processed with most of the beneficial micronutrients (vitamins, minerals, trace elements) cooked out of them. I'm not saying you can NEVER have processed foods, but your priority must always be fresh food to deliver those vital nutrients each day.

ALL ABOUT CALORIES

Ahhhhh calories. Those little critters which we have heard of a million times, and which constantly crop up in articles and government guildelines, can be an easy and effective way for people to track what they are eating.

Calorie counts are particularly useful in the context of pre-prepared foods because a high number of calories will be a hint that this food stuff probably contains a lot of undesirable ingredients such as unhealthy fats, added sugars and processed carbohydrates. Be careful with your counting, however. You could have 100 calories worth of broccoli or 100 calories worth of chocolate. Same

number of calories, two MASSIVELY different impacts upon our biochemistry.

Remember, our body needs energy to run. Have you ever had a completely crazy day at work where you just didnt get a chance to eat all day? At the end of the day were you running around shouting, 'Yippee, I feel as sprightly as a school boy'? No, you probably felt completely and utterly exhausted and away with the fairies, and needed to consume an entire coffee plantation in order to keep going. Your body wasn't getting the fuel that it needed to function, so guess what it started to do? It started to conserve its resources by attempting to REDUCE your activity levels. It made you sluggish and fatigued, made your brain's sparks fizzle out a little. It dulled your ability to do the more taxing activities.

When we lose weight we ARE burning more than we are storing BUT it's important to remember this is to do with fuel *quality*. A fire wouldn't burn hotter and more ferociously with less logs on it, would it? Add more, better-quality firewood and you allow the fire to burn bright! When you adopt better eating patterns and learn how to fuel your body properly, like magic the body's fuel efficiency improves and it can burn what it takes in.

If you want long-term change and most importantly long-term HEALTH, you need to focus on building a healthy diet, not ticking a numbers box. A low-calorie diet won't help you see your 90th birthday. But a diet built around whole foods, high-quality proteins, healthy fats and lots of plant foods? That, my friends, is the path to a long, healthy life.

HOW TO USE THIS BOOK

These recipes are designed to deliver balanced nutrition: hefty amounts of key vitamins, minerals, healthy fats, protein, slow-release carbohydrates, fibre – all the ingredients for a lifelong healthy diet.

You can follow a healthy-eating lifestyle by picking and choosing recipes from anywhere in the book – they are all super easy, quick and realistic for everyday families. You'll find Nutrition Nuggets strewn throughout the recipes to help guide you towards what is good about the dish or a particular ingredient.

There are plenty of options for keen appetites and fussy eaters, and there's a whole chapter of plant-based recipes for vegetarians and vegans.

As we explore in the TV series, a bit of time spent meal planning and batch cooking can really make a difference to how much time and money you can save. For that reason, there are 8 weekly planners at the back of the book which you can follow if you'd like more of a guided programme.

By the end of the 8 weeks, you'll see just how easy it is to eat healthily for the long term. You'll have perfected a collection of recipes that you can turn to again and again, or even add new twists to. As the families in the TV series prove, if you continue to follow the programme, the results can be truly life-changing.

EAT SHOP SAVE SUCCESS STORIES

Everyone that took part in the show lost weight. But it wasn't just the show that people benefited from. We received literally hundreds of emails from people who followed the plan in the first book and, not only did they lose weight, they experienced amazing improvements to their health.

Here are a couple of success stories.

THE BASSETTS

The second series started with the Bassetts, a family from County Durham who were addicted to kebabs. Not only did the family of four slash their shopping bill by 50 per cent in the 8 weeks of filming, they've continued to save since filming and are now looking to book a family holiday. Dan Bassett, a supervisor in a timber yard and dad of the family, was eating pies and sausage rolls for his lunch followed by kebab meat and chips for his dinner before the *Eat Shop Save* team of experts got their hands on the whole family. Luckily, he has changed his habits for the better and has lost an incredible 4 stone in 9 months! He says:

'We do our planner each week using recipes from the *Eat Shop Save* cookbook – it's our bible – then Fiona gets the shopping in. Our bill never goes over £40 a week. We've been able to put away massive savings!

I've not eaten a kebab since filming. I'm not interested one bit. Dale's sausage and chickpea hotpot is my favourite dinner now and we're all still doing the exercises as a family. I bought a multi gym at Christmas and I've used it every day since. I've traded in the kebabs for a six pack...that's my aim anyway!

'Our family life is a hundred per cent better since adopting this new lifestyle without a shadow of a doubt. The food I was eating before was making me poorly, bad-tempered and moody. But now everyone is happy to see me when I come through the door – it's brought us closer as a family unit, it's changed our whole lifestyle.'

THE GREENS

Single mum of two Beccy Green from Greater Manchester has also carried on with her newfound healthy, cash-saving lifestyle since series two ended.

Beccy was very disorganized when it came to her shopping and was visiting the supermarkets around five times a week, with her spending out of control!

'I don't buy whoopsies just for the sake of it any more and I always go shopping with a list, knowing what I already have in so I don't buy double. On average I spend about £30 to £40 a week on my shopping when before I was spending about £125!'

Beccy has got so good at saving, she was able to take her twin girls on a holiday to Wales last year, something which she said would have been near impossible to achieve with their old lifestyle.

Not only has Beccy been making really positive changes to her shopping habits, but the family's overall health has improved dramatically.

'Our favourite food to eat is healthy chicken wraps. The girls will get involved and I will make a homemade salsa to go with them. It's definitely our family favourite – as well as the famous frittata, of course!'

And the results keep on coming, with Beccy reporting dropping FIVE DRESS SIZES since living the *Eat Shop Save* lifestyle. Beccy, who was a size 24, is now wearing size 14–16 clothes.

'I've got so much more energy and I feel so good about myself. I still can't get it into my head that I've lost this much weight – I think because losing weight has always been such a struggle for me and this way of life is just so easy, it's not even sunk in.'

SOUPS & SMOOTHIES

CHAPTER
1

Soups and smoothies are, in my opinion, key ways in which you can pack a lot of goodness into a very small serving. Sipping a smoothie between meals or having a soup as a starter really helps to give your daily food intake a nutritional boost.

One word of guidance about smoothies, though. If you are using a lot of fruit in them, I strongly urge you to make sure you include a good source of protein, which acts to slow down the release of the sugars. The central issue with smoothies isn't necessarily the amount of sugar they contain; it's more how rapidly they raise blood sugar levels. By causing huge spikes in blood sugar, they can sometimes deplete our energy and also increase the risk of weight gain by stimulating a surge in the release of insulin into the bloodstream. The simple solution is to add a high-protein yogurt or nut butter, or go the whole hog and get a protein powder that you can whizz in along with the other ingredients.

High-street chain soup
500 calories per portion
15g fat
4.5g salt

Dale's soup
Average 220 calories per portion
5g fat
1.5g salt

SAVE

Making your own soup is not only incredibly easy, but can be much cheaper (not to mention healthier) than buying it from a high-street chain.

» **Average cost of soup from a chain = £3.50**
» **Average cost of Dale's soup = £0.75**

If you had soup twice a week for lunch from a chain, you'd be spending around £336 a year, compared to around £84 a year if you made it yourself.

This would be a saving of over £250!

BEETROOT AND HORSERADISH SOUP

If you haven't tried this flavour combination, do give it a go – this could become one of your new favourite taste sensations.

4 SERVES | 15 PREP | 20 COOK | 171 CALORIES

OLIVE OIL

1 LARGE RED ONION, FINELY CHOPPED

2 GARLIC CLOVES, FINELY CHOPPED

4 X 250G VACUUM PACKS COOKED BEETROOT (NOT THE PICKLED KIND), DRAINED AND JUICES RESERVED, ROUGHLY CHOPPED

800ML VEGETABLE STOCK

5 TABLESPOONS HORSERADISH SAUCE

SALT

Heat a little olive oil in a large saucepan, add the red onion and garlic along with a good pinch of salt and sauté until the onion has softened.

Add the beetroot and its juices and the vegetable stock and simmer for 10–12 minutes.

Stir in 4 tablespoons of the horseradish sauce. Then using a stick blender, or transferring to a regular blender, blitz the soup until smooth and vibrantly coloured.

Divide between 4 bowls and finish with a swirl of the remaining horseradish.

GINGERED SQUASH SOUP

A classic combination: the sweetness of the squash and the zing of the ginger make such an amazing contrast in this soup. It's a taste explosion!

4 SERVES | 15 PREP | 25 COOK | 182 CALORIES

OLIVE OIL

1 LARGE RED ONION, FINELY CHOPPED

3 GARLIC CLOVES, FINELY CHOPPED

5CM PIECE OF FRESH ROOT GINGER, PEELED AND FINELY CHOPPED

1KG BUTTERNUT SQUASH, SKIN ON, DESEEDED AND DICED

800ML VEGETABLE STOCK

SALT AND PEPPER

Heat a little olive oil in a large saucepan, add the red onion, garlic and ginger along with a good pinch of salt and sauté until the onion has softened.

Add the diced squash and vegetable stock and simmer gently for about 20 minutes until the squash is tender and breaks apart easily when pressed against the side of the pan with a fork.

Using a stick blender, or transferring to a regular blender, blitz the soup until smooth. Divide between 4 bowls and serve with a sprinkling of pepper..

VIBRANT VICHYSSOISE

Vichyssoise is one of those all-time classics that is adored by everyone, which definitely includes me. My version takes the already goodness-packed recipe and gives it even more nutritional value. As with most soups, this freezes well.

4 SERVES | 15 PREP | 30 COOK | 151 CALORIES

OLIVE OIL

1 LARGE ONION, FINELY CHOPPED

3 GARLIC CLOVES, FINELY CHOPPED

300G LEEKS, TRIMMED, CLEANED AND SLICED

110G POTATO, PEELED AND DICED

600ML VEGETABLE STOCK

3 LARGE HANDFULS OF CURLY KALE

6 TABLESPOONS GARDEN PEAS (FRESH OR FROZEN)

SALT AND PEPPER

Heat a little olive oil in a large saucepan, add the onion, garlic and leeks along with a good pinch of salt and sauté until the onion and leeks have softened.

Add the diced potato and vegetable stock and simmer for about 15 minutes until the potato is tender and breaks apart easily when pressed against the side of the pan with a fork.

Using a stick blender, or transferring to a regular blender, blitz the soup until smooth. Add extra water at this point if required.

If you've used a regular blender, return the blended soup to the pan, add the kale and peas and simmer for 3–4 minutes until just cooked. Finish with some black pepper before serving.

NUTRITION NUGGET

In the first *Eat Shop Save* book I showed you how to give your favourites a facelift, and you can apply the same principle to classic dishes to give them a nutritional upgrade, as I've done here with the kale and peas. Always look for ways to pimp up anything you are cooking to add more of the good stuff.

THREE MUSHROOM SOUP

When I first went into nutrition, one of my early obsessions was mushrooms, which might sound dodgy on the face of it, but there are certain varieties of mushroom that can have some incredibly positive influences on immunity. They are also a great source of vitamin D.

4 SERVES
15 PREP
20 COOK
116 CALORIES

OLIVE OIL

1 LARGE ONION, FINELY CHOPPED

3 GARLIC CLOVES, FINELY CHOPPED

150G WHITE MUSHROOMS, SLICED

150G CHESTNUT MUSHROOMS, SLICED

150G SHIITAKE MUSHROOMS, SLICED

1 TABLESPOON PLAIN FLOUR

750ML VEGETABLE STOCK

SALT AND PEPPER

Heat a little olive oil in a large saucepan, add the onion and garlic along with a good pinch of salt and sauté until the onion has softened.

Add all the mushrooms and cook for 3–4 minutes until they are starting to soften and are almost cooked. Remove some of the mushrooms at this point and continue to saute in a separate pan until cooked through. Set aside.

In the main pan, sprinkle over the flour and stir well. Then pour in the vegetable stock and bring to a simmer, stirring. Continue to simmer for 10–12 minutes.

Using a stick blender, or transferring to a regular blender, blitz the soup to a smooth, silky consistency.

Divide between 4 bowls. Garnish each bowl with the extra mushrooms and some black pepper and serve.

NUTRITION NUGGET

Many mushrooms contain a specialized type of sugar called a polysaccharide, which has been shown to stimulate the immune system. Polysaccharides can increase the numbers of certain kinds of white blood cell and also direct those cell types to the site of infection or damage faster.

DREAMY CREAMY CAULIFLOWER SOUP

I used to think that cauliflower was the devil's food. I couldn't stand it – apart from in a soup. Trust me, its flavour is transformed.

4 SERVES · 15 PREP · 20 COOK · 334 CALORIES

OLIVE OIL

1 LARGE ONION, FINELY CHOPPED

3 GARLIC CLOVES, FINELY CHOPPED

800G CAULIFLOWER, CHOPPED

600ML VEGETABLE STOCK

400ML CAN COCONUT MILK

SALT AND PEPPER

Heat a little olive oil in a large saucepan, add the onion and garlic along with a good pinch of salt and sauté until the onion has softened.

Add the cauliflower and vegetable stock and simmer for 10 minutes. Then add the coconut milk and simmer for a further 2–3 minutes until the cauliflower is tender.

Using a stick blender, or transferring to a regular blender, blitz the soup to a smooth, velvety consistency. Divide between 4 bowls and finish with some black pepper.

ROASTED CARROT AND CAULIFLOWER SOUP

The pre-roasting of the veg here brings an extra flavour dimension.

4 SERVES · 15 PREP · 35 COOK · 183 CALORIES

400G CARROTS, CHOPPED

400G CAULIFLOWER FLORETS

OLIVE OIL

1 TEASPOON GROUND CUMIN

1 TEASPOON FENNEL SEEDS, PLUS EXTRA TO SERVE

1 LARGE RED ONION, FINELY CHOPPED

3 GARLIC CLOVES, FINELY CHOPPED

750ML VEGETABLE STOCK

SALT

Preheat the oven to 180°C/160°C fan/Gas Mark 4. Place the carrots and cauliflower in a roasting tin, drizzle with olive oil and toss together well. Sprinkle over the ground cumin and fennel seeds and toss well again to ensure that all the veg are coated. Roast for 20–25 minutes.

Meanwhile, heat a little olive oil in a large saucepan, add the red onion and garlic along with a good pinch of salt and sauté until the onion has softened. Add the roasted carrots and cauliflower and the vegetable stock and simmer for 10 minutes.

Using a stick blender, or transferring to a regular blender, blitz the soup until smooth. Divide between 4 bowls and sprinkle over some extra fennel seeds before serving.

SWEET POTATO AND APPLE SOUP

This combo may sound weird, but my word does it work well! It makes a seriously satisfying soup that is truly unforgettable.

4 SERVES | **15** PREP | **25** COOK | **290** CALORIES

OLIVE OIL

1 LARGE RED ONION, FINELY CHOPPED

2 GARLIC CLOVES, FINELY CHOPPED

800G SWEET POTATOES, SKIN ON, DICED

750ML VEGETABLE STOCK

1 LARGE GREEN APPLE, CORED AND DICED

SALT

Heat a little olive oil in a large saucepan, add the red onion and garlic along with a good pinch of salt and sauté until the onion has softened.

Add the diced sweet potato and the vegetable stock and simmer for about 15 minutes until the sweet potato is tender and breaks apart when pressed against the side of the pan with a fork. Stir in the diced apple and simmer for a further 2–3 minutes.

Using a stick blender, or transferring to a regular blender, blitz the soup until smooth. Divide between 4 bowls and serve.

TOMATO AND WHITE BEAN SOUP

This soup is such a doddle to make (and so speedy, it's hardly worth making extra for freezing), besides being as cheap as chips by using everyday ingredients. It's also packed with antioxidants and minerals.

2 SERVES | **10** PREP | **15** COOK | **348** CALORIES

OLIVE OIL

1 LARGE RED ONION, FINELY CHOPPED

3 GARLIC CLOVES, FINELY CHOPPED

400G CAN TOMATOES

200ML VEGETABLE STOCK

400G CAN CANNELLINI BEANS, DRAINED

SALT

CHOPPED BASIL OR PARSLEY, TO GARNISH (OPTIONAL)

Heat a little olive oil in a saucespan, add the red onion and garlic along with a good pinch of salt and sauté until the onion has softened.

Add the canned tomatoes and vegetable stock and simmer for 3–4 minutes.

Using a stick blender, or transferring to a regular blender, blitz the soup until smooth. If you've used a regular blender, return the blended soup to the pan, add the beans and heat through before serving. Garnish with basil or parsley, if using.

ALL THE BLUES

You might be a bit sceptical about this combination of ingredients, but trust me it's delicious. One word of warning here, though...DO NOT get the cooked beetroot in vinegar or this is going to be one vile experience. But get the unpickled cooked beetroot and all will be grand.

Place all the ingredients in a blender and blitz into a brightly coloured smoothie.

40G BLUEBERRIES

40G BLACKBERRIES

30G COOKED BEETROOT, DICED

70ML NATURAL YOGURT

70ML APPLE JUICE

NUTRITION NUGGET
This smoothie is packed to the hilt with flavonoids, which are part of the chemistry responsible for the deep blue and purple colour pigments of the berries and beet. These have been widely studied and shown to lower blood pressure, protect the insides of blood vessels from damage and also enhance circulation.

MANGO PEACH

This is one of my absolute favourite fruit flavour combinations, with a summery refreshing zing. It's also loaded with so much good stuff.

Place all the ingredients in a blender and blitz into a luscious smoothie.

120G FROZEN MANGO

1 LARGE RIPE PEACH, STONED AND CHOPPED

130ML NATURAL YOGURT

JUICE OF ½ LEMON

NUTRITION NUGGET
Mangoes are a great source of beta carotene, which gives their flesh its orange colour. Beta carotene helps support the healthy condition of the skin, eyes, heart and circulatory system.

PIÑA NO LADA

In my opinion, the classic flavour combination of pineapple and coconut is pretty hard to beat.

Place all the ingredients in a blender and, you've guessed it, blitz into a thick smoothie.

150G PEELED AND DICED FRESH OR FROZEN PINEAPPLE

200ML COCONUT MILK

1 HEAPED TABLESPOON NATURAL YOGURT OR, EVEN BETTER, COCONUT YOGURT

NUTRITION NUGGET
Pineapple contains a powerful enzyme called bromelain, which studies have shown to have some quite powerful anti-inflammatory properties.

SPINACH AND BANANA

This is one of the best smoothies for anyone new to adding vegetables to smoothies. The idea of drinking something made from spinach can put people off, even if they are fully aware of how much good it will do them. You need to trust me here when I say that this mix, while vivid green in colour, only tastes of fruit. Go on...be adventurous!

Place all the ingredients in a blender and blitz for 2 minutes. The spinach does take a little longer to blend but there is nothing worse than spinach strands floating about in the drink!

3 HANDFULS OF BABY SPINACH

1 BANANA, PEELED

200ML APPLE JUICE

1 SCOOP OF VANILLA PROTEIN POWDER (OPTIONAL, BUT FINISHES IT OFF WELL)

NUTRITION NUGGET
This smoothie is a vitamin C bomb, beause spinach contains five to six times the vitamin C of citrus fruit. Most people think of oranges as the ultimate vitamin C source, but salad vegetables like spinach and peppers beat them hands down!

SALADS

CHAPTER

2

Salads may well be the healthy-eating stereotype, but I want to show you that salad doesn't have to mean a manky piece of iceberg lettuce with a dollop of salad cream and a gut full of misery. I am a massive advocate of making one meal a day, usually lunch, a salad-based meal, and once you see some of the incredible combinations that follow, you will discover how insanely good they can actually be.

So what's so special about a salad anyway and why am I such a supporter of a salad a day? Well, it's very simple. It gives you an opportunity to devour as many minimally processed plant foods as you can in a single sitting, and that's a real aspiration for everyone. There is nothing wrong whatsoever with cooking plant foods and some aspects of their nutritional value are even increased or enhanced by cooking. And here, the key is to prepare and cook them in ways that keep any damage to their inherent goodness to a minimum, such as gentle sautéeing. But the ideal is eat a good amount of plant foods raw, which ensures that many of their delicate nutrients such as vitamin C and some of the more fragile phytochemicals and beneficial substances remain unharmed and get delivered to your body intact.

It's all about what you do with those precious plant foods that makes the difference, in terms of both optimum nutrition and enjoyment.

THE EAT SHOP SAVE WAY

Chicken Caesar salad in a restaurant =
850 calories per portion
50g fat
5.9g sugar
2.7 salt

Kale, Parmesan, Chicken and
Anchovy Salad (page 42) =
360 calories per portion
20g fat
3.4g sugar
1.9g salt

Additional benefits include:
» 30% of our recommended daily calcium

NUTRITION NUGGET

Kale is an excellent source of vitamins K, A and C, as well as the minerals calcium, iron, manganese and copper. Kale is, in fact, part of the cruciferous family, along with broccoli and cauliflower. Cruciferous vegetables have many health benefits, one of which includes being helpful for liver detoxification. Kale is also high in antioxidant and anti-inflammatory compounds. All in all, kale is one of the healthiest vegetables around!

It's not just the kale in this delicious dish which delivers a good portion of our daily recommended calcium. It may surprise you, but anchovies are also rich in this mineral. And not only calcium: anchovies also contain anti-inflammatory omega-3 fatty acids; selenium, which plays a key role in metabolism and detoxification; and vitamin A, which is essential for eye health, skin health and the immune system.

ROASTED RED ONION, BEETROOT AND GOATS' CHEESE SALAD

This is a flavour combination that I absolutely adore. You can prep the onions ahead of time so that you can just throw this salad together when you fancy it. Having said that, I personally prefer it when the onions are warm, as they contrast with the goats' cheese beautifully.

2 SERVES · 15 PREP · 30 COOK · 334 CALORIES

1 RED ONION, CUT INTO WEDGES

OLIVE OIL

1 TEASPOON CLEAR HONEY

1 TEASPOON BALSAMIC VINEGAR

2 LARGE HANDFULS OF MIXED SALAD LEAVES (THE DARKER THE BETTER)

1 COOKED BEETROOT, DICED

4–5 CHERRY TOMATOES, HALVED

85G SOFT GOATS' CHEESE

FOR THE DRESSING

1 TABLESPOON OLIVE OIL

1 TEASPOON CLEAR HONEY

1 TEASPOON BALSAMIC VINEGAR

½ TEASPOON DRIED MIXED HERBS

Preheat the oven to 180°C/160°C fan/Gas Mark 4.

Place the red onion wedges in a roasting tin, drizzle with a little olive oil and roast for 10–12 minutes.

Remove the tin from the oven, drizzle the half-cooked onion with the honey and balsamic vinegar and mix together well. Return to the oven for 15 minutes, then remove and set aside.

Add the salad leaves, beetroot and tomatoes to a bowl and toss together well.

Dot the roasted onion around the salad and then crumble the goats' cheese over the top. Mix all the dressing ingredients together in a small bowl, then before pour over the salad before serving.

NUTRITION NUGGET
The fat content in the goats' cheese helps the body absorb the fat-soluble substances in the other salad ingredients, such as carotenoids. You may have noticed that most of the recipes in the book use red onions as opposed to regular onions. This is because they pack an extra-special nutritional punch; it's all to do with the beautiful purple colour pigment, which is provided by a group of phytochemicals called flavonoids. These have been shown to lower blood pressure, improve cognitive function and deliver anti-inflammatory activity.

THE FAMOUS KALE SALAD

I know I know, kale salads have become overly associated with the modern
healthy eating movement. But let me tell you, I have prepared this dish
at cooking demos over the years and had the most hardcore vegetable-dodging
teenagers coming back for second and third helpings of it, so that has
to be testament to how good it is. This is the basic version, to which you
can add cooked new potatoes and a whole host of other salad vegetables.

2 SERVES · 15 PREP · 104 CALORIES

3 LARGE HANDFULS OF CURLY KALE,
TOUGH STALKS REMOVED

OLIVE OIL

4–5 CHERRY TOMATOES, HALVED

SALT

FOR THE DRESSING

1 LARGE GARLIC CLOVE,
FINELY CHOPPED

1 SMALL RED CHILLI, FINELY CHOPPED

1 TABLESPOON SMOOTH
PEANUT BUTTER

2 TEASPOONS SOY SAUCE

1 TEASPOON CLEAR HONEY

½ TEASPOON CHINESE
FIVE-SPICE POWDER

ABOUT 2 TABLESPOONS WATER,
IF/AS NEEDED

Place the kale in a bowl, drizzle over a small amount
of olive oil and sprinkle with a good pinch of salt.

This is the fun part. Get your hands in there and
massage the kale until it has wilted and is close to
the texture of cooked kale. Raw kale as it comes
is not pleasant to eat, but this sorts it out a treat.

Add the tomatoes to the kale and set aside.

Mix all the dressing ingredients together in a small
bowl. As peanut butters can vary, add the water, a little
at a time, to get a pourable consistency, and please feel
free to add more water to get it to the right consistency.

Pour the dressing over the salad and toss together
well so that all the kale is coated before serving.

NUTRITION NUGGET
Greens such as kale are very rich in vitamin K –
a vital nutrient for blood clotting that also helps
support bone health.

FIG AND FETA SALAD

A little beauty that has summer written all over it, this is a glorious collision of sweet and salty that's perfect as a main dish or served as an accompaniment to a barbecue.

3 HANDFULS OF BABY SPINACH

½ COURGETTE

½ RED ONION, SLICED

2 FRESH FIGS, CUT INTO QUARTERS LENGTHWAYS

80G FETA CHEESE

FOR THE DRESSING

1 TABLESPOON OLIVE OIL

1 TABLESPOON GREEK YOGURT

1 TEASPOON LEMON JUICE

½ TEASPOON DRIED OREGANO OR MIXED DRIED HERBS

SALT AND PEPPER

Place the baby spinach on or in a serving plate or bowl.

Cut the courgette into long thin ribbons by running a vegetable peeler down its length. Arrange the courgette ribbons among the spinach.

Add the onion slices and fig quarters.

Mix all the dressing ingredients together in a small bowl, pour over the salad and toss together well to make sure everything is coated.

Crumble over the feta just before serving.

NUTRITION NUGGET
Figs are little powerhouses. They are an excellent source of fibre, which supports digestive and cardiovascular health and keeps us feeling full. Figs are also rich in calcium and antioxidant flavonoids.

CLASSIC NIÇOISE SALAD

The Niçoise is one of those timeless recipes that just never becomes tired or goes out of fashion. You will find this ultimate classic salad on most summer menus, but it's one that's easy to re-create at home.

1 SERVES | 15 PREP | 15 COOK | 809 CALORIES

3 NEW POTATOES

1 EGG

SMALL HANDFUL OF GREEN BEANS

1 LITTLE GEM LETTUCE OR ½ COS LETTUCE, TORN

2 LARGE TOMATOES, QUARTERED

60G DRAINED CANNED TUNA

4 ANCHOVY FILLETS

6–7 PITTED BLACK OLIVES

FOR THE DRESSING

50ML OLIVE OIL

1 TABLESPOON RED WINE VINEGAR

½ TEASPOON DIJON MUSTARD

1 GARLIC CLOVE, FINELY CHOPPED

Place the new potatoes in a small saucepan, cover with boiling water and cook at a rolling boil for 10–12 minutes until just tender. Drain and leave to cool, then cut into quarters.

While the potatoes are cooking, bring a saucepan of water to the boil, carefully drop the egg in and boil for 10 minutes until hard-boiled. About halfway through the egg cooking time, add the green beans to the water.

Once the egg cooking time is up, drain the egg and beans and run both under cold water until the egg is cool enough to handle and the beans are cooled. Shell the egg and leave to cool completely, then cut the cooled egg into quarters.

To assemble the salad, arrange the lettuce on or in your serving plate or bowl first. Top with the tomatoes and potatoes, then the tuna, then the green beans, then the anchovies and finally the olives.

Whisk the dressing ingredients together well before smothering the salad with the dressing.

NUTRITION NUGGET
Many people automatically think of salmon and mackerel as our main sources of omega-3 fatty acids, which they are, but flavoursome little anchovies are packed full too!

KALE, PARMESAN, CHICKEN AND ANCHOVY SALAD

This little bad boy is an absolute flavour bomb. With this much protein, fibre and healthy fats, it's super satisfying too, so you won't be reaching for the snack drawer later in the day.

1 SERVES | **15** PREP | **25** COOK | **360** CALORIES

1 SKINLESS CHICKEN BREAST

2 LARGE HANDFULS OF CURLY KALE, TOUGH STALKS REMOVED

OLIVE OIL

4–5 CHERRY TOMATOES, HALVED

1 CELERY STICK, CUT INTO BATONS

1 TABLESPOON GRATED PARMESAN CHEESE

5–6 ANCHOVY FILLETS

SALT AND PEPPER

Preheat the oven to 180°C/160°C fan/Gas Mark 4.

Place the chicken breast on a baking tray, season with a little salt and pepper and bake for 20–25 minutes until cooked through.

Meanwhile, place the kale in a bowl, drizzle with olive oil and sprinkle with a pinch of salt. Get your hands in the bowl and massage the kale until it has wilted and is close to the texture of cooked kale.

Add the tomatoes, celery and Parmesan and mix together until the Parmesan is clinging to all the ingredients.

Plate up the salad, then top with the anchovies. Cut the chicken breast into bite-sized slices and fan these out on the top of the salad.

NUTRITION NUGGET
The kale in this recipe contains almost twice as much calcium as the Parmesan cheese does. So don't always assume that dairy products are the ultimate source of this vital mineral.

GOATS' CHEESE AND ROASTED VEGETABLE SALAD

A firm favourite in my house, this gorgeous salad is at its best served warm, but the roasted veggies will keep perfectly well in the fridge for adding cold to a salad the next day, or as a great sandwich filler with some hummus.

2 SERVES · 20 PREP · 40 COOK · 400 CALORIES

1 LARGE RED ONION,
CUT INTO WEDGES

1 LARGE COURGETTE,
CUT INTO ROUNDS

1 LARGE RED PEPPER, CORED,
DESEEDED AND DICED

2-3 CHESTNUT MUSHROOMS, SLICED

OLIVE OIL

2 TEASPOONS SMOKED PAPRIKA

2/3 TEASPOON GARLIC SALT

1 TEASPOON DRIED MIXED HERBS

3 LARGE HANDFULS OF
MIXED SALAD LEAVES

160G GOATS' CHEESE LOG,
CUT INTO EQUAL-SIZED ROUNDS

Preheat the oven to 180°C/160°C fan/Gas Mark 4.

Place all the vegetables in a roasting tin, drizzle with a little olive oil and toss together well so that they are all coated. Sprinkle over the smoked paprika, garlic salt and dried herbs, and mix well again to ensure that the seasoning clings to all the veg.

Roast the veg for about 40 minutes, stirring once or twice. You want them to be soft and beginning to caramelize. Drain any cooking juices that accumulate in the tin and reserve for later.

Preheat the grill and line a baking tray with foil.

Divide the salad leaves between 2 serving plates, then scatter over the warm roasted veg.

Lay the rounds of goats' cheese on the foil-lined tray and place under the grill for 30–45 seconds only, just to warm up and soften the top layer.

Top each salad with the warmed rounds of goats' cheese. Drizzle any reserved roasted vegetable juices over the salad as a dressing.

NUTRITION NUGGET
Using the cooking juices means that you don't miss out on the benefits of some of the nutrients that may have leached out in the roasting process.

QUINOA, PEA, MINT AND FETA SALAD WITH LIME DRESSING

This salad has a beautiful summer vibe to it, and it's another that is just as happy as a side as it is a main course.

1 SERVES | 15 PREP | 20 COOK | 481 CALORIES

35G QUINOA

35G FROZEN PEAS

5CM PIECE OF CUCUMBER, DICED

10G MINT LEAVES, TORN

85G FETA CHEESE

FOR THE DRESSING

JUICE OF 1 LIME

1 TABLESPOON OLIVE OIL

¼ TEASPOON GARLIC SALT

Place the quinoa in a saucepan, cover with boiling water and simmer for 20 minutes, or until it has softened and appears to have developed little tails.

Add the frozen peas for the last 3–4 minutes of the quinoa cooking time.

Once the quinoa cooking time is up, drain the quinoa and peas and transfer to a bowl. Add the cucumber and mint and mix together well.

Crumble in the feta and mix well again.

Whisk the dressing ingredients together well before dressing the salad.

NUTRITION NUGGET
Quinoa is one of the most nutrient-dense grains on the planet. With an impressive array of vitamins and minerals, it's also a great protein source, because it contains all nine essential amino acids.

PEACH, BLUE CHEESE AND WATERCRESS SALAD

Ok...I've gone into the weird zone again. Believe me, though, when I say that this is a salad to impress. Bring this out at a barbecue and, once your friends have finished scratching their heads in bewilderment, they will take one taste and get their minds blown. It's worth making just for the reaction! I say making, but this salad is simply an assembly job.

1 SERVES

10 PREP

427 CALORIES

1 LARGE PEACH, STONED AND SLICED

GENEROUS HANDFUL OF WATERCRESS

2 TABLESPOONS NATURAL YOGURT

65G STRONG BLUE CHEESE

SALT AND PEPPER

Mix the peach slices and watercress together on a plate.

Add the yogurt to a ramekin. Crumble in the blue cheese with a little salt and pepper and mix together well.

Smother the salad with the blue cheese dressing before serving.

NUTRITION NUGGET
Peaches are a great source of vitamin C, beta carotene, potassium and manganese.

THAI-STYLE VEGGIE 'NOODLE' SALAD

It's official...vegetable noodles have become 'a thing'. I have had one of those spiralizer contraptions since the 1990s – back then we were mavericks! But now, thanks to the huge popularity of veggie noodles, you no longer have to grapple with such a gadget because they are available pre-prepared in your supermarket. Winner!

1 SERVES

10 PREP

312 CALORIES

HANDFUL OF PRE-PREPARED CARROT NOODLES

HANDFUL OF PRE-PREPARED COURGETTE NOODLES

20G CORIANDER

1 TABLESPOON CASHEW NUTS

SALT

FOR THE DRESSING

JUICE OF 1 LIME

2 TEASPOONS SOY SAUCE

2 TEASPOONS OLIVE OIL

1 TEASPOON SESAME OIL

1 GARLIC CLOVE, VERY FINELY CHOPPED

½ RED CHILLI, FINELY CHOPPED (OPTIONAL)

Place the carrot and courgette noodles in a bowl, add the coriander and toss together until evenly combined.

Whisk all the dressing ingredients together well before pouring over the noodles. Toss well again to ensure everything is evenly coated before plating up.

Place the cashews in a folded clean tea towel and give them a wallop with a rolling pin or similar blunt instrument to crush them coarsely. Sprinkle the cashews over the salad and season with a little salt.

NUTRITION NUGGET
Cashew nuts are a great source of calcium, magnesium, zinc, vitamin E and protein.

SMOKED MACKEREL, WATERCRESS AND COURGETTE SALAD WITH AVOCADO HORSERADISH DRESSING

This is a flavour fest and no mistake, containing an enormous array of nutrients. The dressing is quite something too – vivid green and bursting with fiery, zingy flavour.

1 SERVES | **15 PREP** | **905 CALORIES**

LARGE HANDFUL OF WATERCRESS

1 COURGETTE

1 SMOKED MACKEREL FILLET

FOR THE DRESSING

1 VERY RIPE AVOCADO, STONED AND PEELED

JUICE OF 1 LEMON

2 HEAPED TEASPOONS HOT HORSERADISH SAUCE

1 TABLESPOON OLIVE OIL

SALT AND PEPPER

Place all the dressing ingredients, along with a splash of water, in a food processor or blender and blitz into a smooth dressing.

Arrange the watercress on a plate.

Cut the courgette into long thin ribbons by running a vegetable peeler down its length. Arrange the courgette ribbons among the watercress.

Flake the mackerel over the salad, discarding any skin.

Pour the dressing over the salad before serving.

NUTRITION NUGGET
Fresh horseradish root was traditionally used medicinally to tackle colds and coughs. Just eat a piece and you will see how quickly it can clear the airways!

BEAN AND BEETROOT SALAD WITH ROCKET AND PESTO

This is an absolute belter of a salad! I'm slightly obsessed with the beetroot and pesto combo.

2 SERVES | 10 PREP | 330 CALORIES

Place the beetroot and cannellini beans in a bowl.

1 LARGE COOKED BEETROOT, DICED

400G CAN CANNELLINI BEANS, DRAINED

2 HEAPED TABLESPOONS PESTO

2 HANDFULS OF ROCKET

SALT AND PEPPER

OLIVE OIL AND LEMON JUICE, TO SERVE (OPTIONAL)

Add the pesto and stir together until well coated.

Add the rocket and toss together gently, then season with a little salt and pepper to taste before plating up.

You can add a drizzle of olive oil and lemon juice to the salad once plated to give it an extra zing.

HERBED CHICKPEA AND OLIVE SALAD

This super-filling salad is a winner for lunch when you're in a rush.

2 SERVES | 15 PREP | 431 CALORIES

Place all the salad ingredients in a bowl and mix together well. Season with a little salt and pepper to taste.

400G CAN CHICKPEAS, DRAINED

6–7 CHERRY TOMATOES, HALVED

2 TABLESPOONS PITTED KALAMATA OLIVES, CHOPPED

40G PARSLEY, ROUGHLY CHOPPED

½ AVOCADO, PEELED AND DICED

SALT AND PEPPER

FOR THE DRESSING

1 TABLESPOON OLIVE OIL

1 TEASPOON BRINE FROM THE OLIVES

1 TEASPOON LEMON JUICE

1 TEASPOON BALSAMIC VINEGAR

Mix all the dressing ingredients together in a small bowl. Pour over the salad and toss together well before serving.

NUTRITION NUGGET
Parsley is an incredibly rich source of vitamin C and is packed with aromatic oils that are reputed to ease bloating and gas.

MEAT

CHAPTER
3

We seem to be in a time now where meat is regarded as something unhealthy, and some pieces of research linking the consumption of processed meats like smoked bacon with disease have caused many to hold the belief that all meat can negatively impact our health. This certainly isn't true. If you choose to eat meat, there is a great deal of nutritional value that can be found in it.

Red meat is an excellent source of many minerals such as iron, zinc and selenium, not to mention vitamins A and D. In fact, the iron in red meat, haem iron, is more easily absorbed than non-haem iron from plant sources.

Chicken and turkey are not only excellent protein sources but they can also contain many nutrients. All B vitamins are present in chicken and turkey meat, including B1, B2, B3, B5, B6, B12, folate and choline. They are a particularly good source of vitamin B3; one serving can provide almost all of our recommended daily intake. When it comes to minerals, they are particularly rich in selenium and also contain good amounts of zinc, copper, phosphorus, magnesium and iron.

So if you've been avoiding meat in the name of good health, this chapter will be good news for you!

Chinese sweet and sour chicken from a takeaway =
over 1,000 calories per portion
over 50g fat
over 7g salt

Chicken with Spring Onions in Satay Sauce (page 74) =
282 calories per portion
11g fat
0.85g salt

NUTRITION NUGGET

This dish is a great source of the sulphur-rich vegetables garlic, onion and spring onions. These are not only important for liver health but they also contain prebiotics that can be incredibly beneficial for the good bacteria in our gut.

Did you know that peanuts are not actually nuts but legumes? They are an excellent source of biotin, a B-complex vitamin that has an important role in blood sugar balance and skin health. Peanuts are also a very good source of copper as well as a good source of manganese, vitamin B1, niacin (vitamin B3), molybdenum, folate, vitamin E, phosphorus and protein. Peanut butter is high in fat, but do not let this put you off enjoying its many health benefits. In moderation, of course!

WARM STEAK SALAD

This gorgeous dish is perfect for lunch or a summertime evening meal.
It's heaven for me and typical of the sort of fare I reach for regularly.
Although the recipe is for one, it's easy to multiply up.

1 SERVES **10 PREP** **12 COOK** **392 CALORIES**

1 CARROT

2 HANDFULS OF MIXED SALAD LEAVES

SMALL HANDFUL OF ROCKET

SMALL HANDFUL OF CHERRY TOMATOES, QUARTERED

OLIVE OIL

100G OF YOUR PREFERRED CUT OF STEAK – I'M A SIRLOIN FAN PERSONALLY – AT ROOM TEMPERATURE

SALT AND PEPPER

FOR THE DRESSING

1 TEASPOON MAYONNAISE

1 TEASPOON BALSAMIC VINEGAR OR LEMON JUICE

½ TEASPOON ENGLISH MUSTARD

2 TEASPOONS OLIVE OIL

SALT AND PEPPER

Begin by cutting the carrot into long, thin ribbons by running a vegetable peeler down its length. This looks fancy but really is a cinch to do.

Add the carrot ribbons to a bowl with all the leaves and tomatoes and toss together well.

Heat a frying pan until very hot and add a drizzle of olive oil. Season the steak on both sides with salt and pepper and fry according to your preference – 2 minutes on each side for rare, 4 minutes on each side for medium and 5–6 minutes on each side for well done. This is just a guide, as the exact timing will depend on the cut and thickness of the steak, but it hits the average.

Meanwhile, mix all the dressing ingredients together in a small bowl. They may separate a little if left to stand, but this is normal and a quick stir will sort it out.

Slice the steak into thin strips, add to the salad and toss well. Drizzle the dressing over the top and serve.

NUTRITION NUGGET
When choosing salad vegetables, opt for the darkest and most vivid colours you can find. Each colour represents a different spectrum of nutrients, and the richer the colour, the more of the good stuff is in there.

CHICKEN WITH PEPPERED MUSHROOM SAUCE

An elegant yet comforting dish, this is a total doddle to make, taking very little time at all to knock together.

1 SERVES · **10 PREP** · **30 COOK** · **455 CALORIES**

1 LARGE SKINLESS CHICKEN BREAST

OLIVE OIL

1 GARLIC CLOVE, FINELY CHOPPED

1 ROSEMARY SPRIG (OPTIONAL)

120G MUSHROOMS, SLICED

30G FULL-FAT SOFT CHEESE

2–3 TABLESPOONS WATER

½ TEASPOON COARSELY GROUND BLACK PEPPER

SALT

WILTED GREENS AND SWEET POTATO MASH, TO SERVE

Preheat the oven to 180°C/160°C fan/Gas Mark 4.

Place the chicken breast on a baking tray and bake for 25–30 minutes until cooked through.

Meanwhile, to make the sauce, heat a little olive oil in a frying pan, add the garlic along with a good pinch of salt and sauté over a low heat for 3–4 minutes.

Add the rosemary, if using, and the sliced mushrooms and continue to sauté until the mushrooms soften.

Stir in the soft cheese, measured water and black pepper and simmer for 3–4 minutes. You can add a little more water at this stage to make sure the sauce is a pourable consistency – not too thick, not too thin.

This dish is perfect served with some wilted greens and sweet potato mash. Plate up the accompaniments and the chicken breast, then pour the sauce all over the chicken.

NUTRITION NUGGET
High-quality sources of fat and protein like the soft cheese and chicken here can keep us feeling fuller for longer and control appetite.

SAUSAGE, SAGE AND SQUASH ONE-TRAY ROAST

One-tray roasts and bakes are a beautiful and effortless way to cook, especially in the colder months. The flavours fully develop and fuse together well with areas of inviting caramelization, resulting in something warming and hearty. Lovely!

4 SERVES · **15 PREP** · **40 COOK** · **496 CALORIES**

1 SMALL BUTTERNUT SQUASH, SKIN ON, DESEEDED AND CUBED

OLIVE OIL

8 HIGH-QUALITY PORK SAUSAGES

1 LARGE RED ONION, HALVED AND THICKLY SLICED LENGTHWAYS

15–20G SAGE, ROUGHLY CHOPPED

SALT AND PEPPER

Preheat the oven to 180°C/160°C fan/Gas Mark 4.

Place the squash cubes in a roasting tin, drizzle with a little olive oil and toss together well. Roast for about 10 minutes.

Meanwhile, prick each of the sausages with a fork so that they have a few holes in on both sides.

After 10 minutes, remove the tin of squash from the oven, add the onion slices and mix together well, then lay the pricked sausages on top. Return to the oven for 15 minutes.

Remove the roasting tin from the oven again, add the chopped sage and stir well. Return to the oven for a final 15 minutes.

After the total roasting time of about 40 minutes, the squash should be soft, the sausages cooked through and the onions caramelized.

NUTRITION NUGGET
The vivid orange flesh of the butternut squash is provided by something called beta carotene, the plant form of vitamin A. It supports healthy skin and a healthy heart, and is a potent antioxidant.

BEEF, BROCCOLI AND GINGER STIR-FRY

Stir-fries really are one of the staples of healthier cooking. They give you the opportunity to throw together all manner of amazing fresh ingredients and cook them quickly and in a way that retains many of the beneficial nutrients they contain.

4 SERVES
15 PREP
10 COOK
265 CALORIES

OLIVE OIL

3 GARLIC CLOVES, FINELY CHOPPED

5CM PIECE OF FRESH ROOT GINGER, PEELED AND SLICED INTO VERY THIN, NEEDLE-LIKE LENGTHS

1 LARGE HEAD OF BROCCOLI, CUT INTO SMALL FLORETS

500G PRE-CUT BEEF STRIPS

1 TABLESPOON SESAME OIL

3 TABLESPOONS CHINESE OYSTER SAUCE

SALT

BROWN RICE, TO SERVE

Heat a wok or deep frying pan until hot and add a drizzle of olive oil.

Add the garlic, ginger and broccoli along with a good pinch of salt and stir-fry over a medium-high heat for about 5–6 minutes until the broccoli is beginning to soften and the garlic is fragrant.

Add the beef strips and continue to stir-fry for a further 3–4 minutes.

Add the sesame oil and oyster sauce and a splash of water, then toss together well.

Serve the stir-fry with some brown rice.

NUTRITION NUGGET
Stir-frying is a great method of cooking for preserving many of the fragile water-soluble nutrients such as the B vitamins and vitamin C.

TURKEY STUFFED PEPPERS

This is a wonderfully simple supper idea, and also ideal
for an easy make-ahead lunch.

4 SERVES | 15 PREP | 25 COOK | 252 CALORIES

2 LARGE RED PEPPERS, HALVED,
CORED AND DESEEDED

OLIVE OIL

1 ONION, FINELY CHOPPED

3 GARLIC CLOVES, FINELY CHOPPED

500G TURKEY MINCE

2 TABLESPOONS FULL-FAT
SOFT CHEESE

1 TEASPOON DRIED MIXED HERBS

¼ TEASPOON COARSELY
GROUND BLACK PEPPER

SALT

SALAD AND BROWN RICE
OR QUINOA, TO SERVE

Preheat the oven to 200°C/180°C fan/Gas Mark 6.

Place the red pepper halves cut side down on a baking
tray and bake for 12–15 minutes.

Meanwhile, heat a little olive oil in a large frying pan,
add the onion and garlic along with a good pinch of salt
and sauté until the onion has softened.

Add the turkey mince, breaking it down with the
wooden spoon or spatula, and cook for 5–6 minutes
until golden brown throughout, stirring frequently.

Add the soft cheese, herbs and black pepper and cook
for a further minute or so.

Remove the tray from the oven. Turn the pepper
halves over and divide the turkey mixture between
them, scooping it into the pepper cavities and pressing
it down with the back of the spoon to pack it in.

Bake the stuffed peppers for 10 minutes.

Serve with a salad and brown rice or quinoa.

NUTRITION NUGGET
Red peppers are a good source of carotenoids, which are
responsible for their rich colour. These are fat-soluble
substances, so the cheese in this turkey mixture enhances
their absorption. In short, adding the fat means your
body gets more of the good stuff!

CHINESE ROAST CHICKEN

Blast your Sunday roasts into orbit with this delicious twist on roast chicken!
It does need prepping in advance to achieve that maximum flavour hit.

4 SERVES

10 PREP **8** HOURS CHILL

90 COOK

584 CALORIES

....
1 MEDIUM CHICKEN, ABOUT 1.5KG
....

FOR THE MARINADE

3 TABLESPOONS LIGHT SOY SAUCE

2 TEASPOONS CLEAR HONEY

1 TEASPOON CHINESE
FIVE-SPICE POWDER

1 TEASPOON TOASTED SESAME OIL

¼ TEASPOON SALT

FOR THE GLAZE

1 TABLESPOON OLIVE OIL

1 TEASPOON TOASTED SESAME OIL

1 TEASPOON CLEAR HONEY

Begin by mixing all the marinade ingredients together in a small bowl.

Place the chicken in a large sealable food bag. Pour the marinade into the bag, seal and then shake and/or rotate the bag to make sure the chicken is covered in the marinade. Place in the fridge for about 8 hours (or overnight), rotating or shaking it every few hours so that the marinade doesn't just accumulate in one area.

When ready to cook, preheat the oven to 190°C/170°C fan/Gas Mark 5. Transfer the chicken to a roasting tin, add a good splash of water to the tin and roast for 1 hour.

Remove the tin from the oven. Mix the glaze ingredients together and drizzle all over the chicken.

Return the chicken to the oven and roast for a further 25 minutes (or the remaining cooking time, calculated by weight – 45 minutes per kg plus 20 minutes in total) until cooked through. To test that the chicken is done, slice through the skin where a thigh joins the breast, pierce the thickest part of the thigh with a knife and check that the juices run clear, not pink.

NUTRITION NUGGET
Chicken is a rich source of a substance called carnosine, a dipeptide – two amino acids bound together – that's important for supporting the immune system and the long-term health of many tissues. It is said by some to have an almost 'anti-ageing' effect. While this might be a bit of a stretch, its supportive role for so many tissues means it does have diverse health benefits.

PORK RISSOLES WITH APPLE AND FENNEL PURÉE

This gorgeous dish would be equally perfect for a dinner party or on the Sunday lunch table. It may sound fancy, but it's really simple in practice.

4 SERVES

20 PREP

30 COOK

439 CALORIES

500G PORK MINCE

2 GARLIC CLOVES, FINELY CHOPPED

15G SAGE, ROUGHLY CHOPPED

1 EGG, BEATEN

SALT AND PEPPER

FOR THE PURÉE

1 LARGE FENNEL BULB, SLICED

1 LARGE GREEN APPLE, CORED AND SLICED

1 ONION, SLICED

OLIVE OIL

250ML VEGETABLE STOCK

FOR THE GREENS

GENEROUS KNOB OF BUTTER

200G GARDEN PEAS (FRESH OR FROZEN)

200G CURLY KALE

Begin with the purée. Preheat the oven to 200°C/180°C fan/Gas Mark 6. Place the fennel, apple and onion slices in a roasting tin and drizzle with a little olive oil. Roast for 25–30 minutes. You want all the ingredients to soften and for some caramelization to occur.

Meanwhile, make the rissoles. Place the mince, garlic, sage, egg and some salt and pepper in a bowl, and use your hands to mix together well. Divide the mixture into 4 and form each portion into a large burger-style patty.

Heat a little olive oil in a frying pan and fry the rissoles for 5–6 minutes on each side until cooked through.

Melt the butter in a pan, add the peas and kale and sauté until the peas have softened and the kale has turned brighter green.

Transfer the roasted apple, fennel and onion to a food processor or blender along with the vegetable stock. Blitz at high speed to form a silky purée. If you need to thin the purée down, add a little water. The texture you are aiming for is a very thick soup.

Divide the purée, peas and kale and the rissoles between 4 plates.

NUTRITION NUGGET
Fennel contains essential oils that help to alleviate gas and bloating. Fennel seeds were traditionally used to make a tea to treat infant colic. The oils that give them their distinct fragrance can relax the gut wall and ease bloating, gas and cramps.

CHICKEN WITH SPRING ONIONS IN SATAY SAUCE

An absolute belter of a dish, this has a divine richness. If you have fussy eaters in the house, it can be gold dust

4 SERVES

15 PREP

30 COOK

282 CALORIES

OLIVE OIL

6 GARLIC CLOVES, FINELY CHOPPED

1 RED ONION, HALVED AND SLICED LENGTHWAYS

4 SKINLESS CHICKEN BREASTS, DICED

3 LARGE SPRING ONIONS, SLICED

3 TABLESPOONS PEANUT BUTTER

1 TEASPOON CHINESE FIVE-SPICE POWDER

2 TEASPOONS CLEAR HONEY

2 TEASPOONS SOY SAUCE

SMALL HANDFUL OF CORIANDER LEAVES, ROUGHLY CHOPPED (OPTIONAL)

SALT

BROWN RICE OR WILTED GREENS, TO SERVE

Heat a little olive oil in a frying pan and sauté the garlic and red onion slices along with a good pinch of salt for 3–4 minutes until the onion has started to soften.

Add the diced chicken breasts and cook for a further 7–8 minutes, stirring frequently. Add the spring onions and cook for another 3–4 minutes.

Whisk together the the peanut butter, five-spice powder, honey and soy sauce with a splash of water in a bowl. Add to the pan and cook for 2 minutes. At this stage, cut into the largest chunk of chicken and ensure it is cooked through.

Sprinkle over the chopped coriander, if using, and serve with brown rice or some wilted greens.

NUTRITION NUGGET
Many people are scared of ingredients like peanut butter because they have such a high fat content. From now on, I want you to think of natural high-quality fats as your friend, as they are vital to our health. Sure, the wrong types of fat are very bad indeed, and I cover that in the opening chapters, but good fats provide the building blocks for hormones, can keep you feeling fuller for longer and stabilize blood sugar. It's clear that we are way off base as a nation when it comes to nutrition, so it's time to rethink what we've been previously taught.

HONEY MUSTARD PORK CHOPS WITH KALE AND MUSHROOM SAUTÉ

This is the ideal dish for those who may be a little resistant to healthier food. We have to ease our way in, and a flavoursome dish like this is the perfect way to do that. Personally, I keep any type of added sugar such as honey to an absolute minimum, but I don't expect everyone to leap immediately into complete dietary overhaul.

4 SERVES | 10 PREP | 25 COOK | 355 CALORIES

4 TEASPOONS CLEAR HONEY

2 TEASPOONS ENGLISH MUSTARD

½ TEASPOON GARLIC SALT

4 PORK CHOPS

15G SALTED BUTTER

200G CURLY KALE, ROUGHLY CHOPPED

250G CHESTNUT MUSHROOMS, SLICED

SALT AND PEPPER

Preheat the oven to 200°C/180°C fan/Gas Mark 6.

Mix the honey, mustard and garlic salt together in a large bowl. Add the pork chops to the bowl and mix into the honey and mustard mixture well, ensuring the chops are fully coated with it.

Place the chops on a baking tray and drizzle over any of the honey and mustard mixture left in the bowl. Bake in the oven for 20–25 minutes until well browned and cooked through.

Meanwhile, melt the butter in a pan, add the kale and mushrooms and sauté until the kale has wilted and the mushrooms are soft. Season with a little salt and pepper

Serve the super-tasty pork chops with the sautéed veg.

NUTRITION NUGGET
Kale has become one of those fashionable ingredients that seems to be in every trendy eatery. I'm not sure how a relative of cabbage has become so glamorous, but there we go! The question is...is it any good? Well, yes. It delivers a huge amount of magnesium, vitamin K, vitamin C and sulphur-containing glucosinolates. So it is a great ingredient all round, and cheap as chips too!

HERBED TURKEY MEATBALLS WITH COURGETTE COUSCOUS

There is a wonderful familiarity about this dish that makes it a hit with many a picky eater. You can make extra batches of the raw meatballs to freeze for later use, simply defrosting them before cooking in the sauce. Or try pan-frying for 8–10 minutes and serving with pasta or a salad.

4 SERVES

20 PREP

1 HOUR CHILL

35 COOK

432 CALORIES

500G TURKEY MINCE

1 EGG, BEATEN

2 GARLIC CLOVES, FINELY CHOPPED

2 TEASPOONS DRIED MIXED HERBS

PINCH OF SALT

FOR THE COUSCOUS

1 LARGE COURGETTE, SLICED INTO ROUNDS

1 LARGE RED ONION, HALVED AND THICKLY SLICED LENGTHWAYS

OLIVE OIL

1 TEASPOON SMOKED PAPRIKA

200G COUSCOUS, PREFERABLY WHOLEWHEAT

SALT AND PEPPER

FOR THE SAUCE

OLIVE OIL

½ RED ONION, FINELY CHOPPED

2 GARLIC CLOVES, FINELY CHOPPED

400G CAN CHOPPED TOMATOES

150ML STOCK OR WATER

Place the turkey mince, egg, garlic, mixed herbs and salt in a bowl. Get your hands in there and mix everything together well. Cover and refrigerate for an hour.

Meanwhile, preheat the oven to 200°C/180°C fan/Gas Mark 6. Place the courgette and onion for the couscous on a baking tray. Drizzle over a little olive oil, sprinkle with the paprika and then season. Toss together well. Roast for 20–25 minutes, stirring occasionally.

Meanwhile, make the sauce. Heat a little olive oil in a pan, add the onion and garlic along with a good pinch of salt and cook until the onion has softened. Add the canned tomatoes and stock or water, then simmer for 10–12 minutes, stirring occasionally. Take off the heat.

Remove the turkey mixture from the fridge and roll it into balls about half the size of a golf ball. Place the balls on a baking tray and bake for 15 minutes. Add to the sauce and simmer for 5 minutes.

Place the couscous in a heatproof bowl and pour over an equal volume of boiled water. Cover the bowl with a tea towel and let the couscous sit for 10 minutes until it has absorbed all the water. Fluff up with a fork.

Add the roasted courgette and onion and all residual oil and juices from the tray to the couscous and mix well before serving with the meatballs and sauce.

BEEF AND JALAPEÑO BURGER WITH GUACAMOLE

This bun-free burger is great for anyone following a lower-carbohydrate diet. Having said that, you could, of course, place this in a wholemeal bun, but just be ready with lots of paper napkins to wipe the guacamole off your fingers!

6 SERVES · **20 PREP** · **12 COOK** · **300 CALORIES**

450G MINCED BEEF

4 JALAPEÑO CHILLIES, FINELY CHOPPED

3 GARLIC CLOVES, FINELY CHOPPED

3 TABLESPOONS TOMATO PURÉE

1 TEASPOON GROUND CORIANDER

SALT

SIDE SALAD, TO SERVE

FOR THE GUACAMOLE

2 VERY RIPE AVOCADOS

½ RED ONION, FINELY CHOPPED

2 GARLIC CLOVES, FINELY CHOPPED

1 GREEN CHILLI, FINELY CHOPPED

JUICE OF 1 LIME

SALT

Place the minced beef, jalapeños, garlic, tomato purée, coriander and a good pinch of salt in a bowl and use your hands to mix together well.

Preheat the grill and line a baking tray with foil.

Divide the meat mixture into 3 and form each portion into a burger patty.

Lay the burgers on the foil-lined tray, place under the grill and cook for 5–6 minutes on each side until cooked through.

Meanwhile, make the guacamole. Halve the avocados lengthways and remove the stones. Scoop the avocado flesh into a bowl and mash well with a fork. Add the remaining ingredients and mix together well, then season to taste with salt.

Serve the burgers topped with a huge dollop of guacamole, along with a generous side salad.

NUTRITION NUGGET
Avocados are not only trendy but very good for you, being a great source of oleic acid and vitamin E, which can both benefit heart health.

BEEF AND BEETROOT CASSEROLE

Two of my absolute favourite ingredients brought together in one single dish. You could make this up to three days in advance, cool and keep in the fridge, or freeze all or some for defrosting and reheating another day. It's great served with sweet potato mash.

6 SERVES

15 PREP

1¼ HOURS COOK

390 CALORIES

OLIVE OIL

1KG BRAISING STEAK, CUT INTO ABOUT 4CM PIECES

2 RED ONIONS, FINELY CHOPPED

3 GARLIC CLOVES, FINELY CHOPPED

1 HEAPED TABLESPOON PLAIN FLOUR

300ML RED WINE

200ML BEEF STOCK

1 TABLESPOON CLEAR HONEY

2 CINNAMON STICKS

250G VACUUM PACK COOKED BEETROOT (NOT THE PICKLED KIND), DRAINED AND JUICES RESERVED

SALT AND PEPPER

Preheat the oven to 180°C/160°C fan/Gas Mark 4.

Heat a little olive oil in a large heavy-based saucepan, add the beef, a few pieces at a time, and cook for 2–3 minutes until browned all over. Remove from the pan and set aside.

Add a little more oil to the pan and sauté the red onions and garlic along with a good pinch of salt until the onion has softened. Return all the beef to the pan, sprinkle over the flour and cook for a further 2–3 minutes.

Pour in the wine and stock and bring to a simmer, stirring. Add the honey, cinnamon and a generous seasoning of salt and pepper. Cover the pan and simmer for 1½ hours.

Cut any large beetroot in half and add them to the pan along with the beetroot juices. Re-cover and simmer for another 30 minutes.

NUTRITION NUGGET

While we shouldn't eat red meat every day, consumed once or twice a month it can supply us with excellent amounts of iron, zinc and selenium. Beetroot is rich in nitric oxide, which helps lower blood pressure, as I explain on page 128. It is also very high in fibre and a substance called betacyanin that can help support liver health.

FISH & SEAFOOD

CHAPTER
4

Anyone who has followed my work for any length of time will know that I am a huge fish and seafood advocate. It's one of the number one ingredients for me, for three major reasons.

Firstly, oily fish in particular, such as salmon, tuna, mackerel and sardines, are an amazing source of the all-important omega-3 fatty acids. These are specialized substances derived from fats that have numerous roles to play in the body. They regulate inflammation, which is vitally important for long-term health and for reducing the risk of degenerative disease. They are also a structural material, for example supporting the structure and function of nerve cells and the eyes. You really could fill a book just on the essential health functions that omega-3 fatty acids perform, and these are something I talk about over and over in this book – and in every book I write.

Secondly, fish is also a great source of important minerals and trace elements. Fish and seafood are often rich in the mineral selenium, which helps to raise the levels of our own natural inbuilt antioxidant substances that our cells produce. Many fish are a significant source of zinc, which is key for an effective immune system and skin health, and is a cofactor for hundreds of different enzymes in the body.

Thirdly, fish is a wonderfully easy-to-digest protein source. So, all in all, it's something that we should aim to eat more of. However, people remain apprehensive of it or don't know how to be adventurous with it; hopefully these recipes will show you that it can be versatile, simple to cook with and delicious.

THE EAT SHOP SAV£ WAY

Fish and chips and mushy peas
in a restaurant or takeaway =
up to 1,200 calories per serving
up to 7g salt

River Cobbler with Broad Bean Mash
and Lime Rocket Salad (page 90) =
540 calories per serving
2.4g salt

Additional benefits include:
» Almost 50% of our recommended daily selenium
» 40% of our recommended daily zinc
» Almost 100% of our recommended daily B3 and B5

NUTRITION NUGGET
This vibrant dish is not only much lower in calories and salt than a
typical takeaway fish and chips, it also packs a serious nutritional punch.
Rocket provides numerous health benefits due to its high nutrient
density. The nutrient-packed greens provide substantial amounts of
vitamins A, K and C, folate, calcium, iron, potassium, magnesium and
several beneficial phytochemicals. The minerals in rocket can have a
positive effect on blood pressure, since calcium, magnesium and
potassium all have an important role in helping our blood vessels relax.
Eating bitter foods, such as rocket, before a meal can help to stimulate
our digestive enzymes. Proper digestion of food is important for getting
all the nutrients from our meal.

TUNA AND SWEET POTATO FISH CAKES

These are super simple to make and have a great comfort-food factor to them as well. In short, an easy family favourite revisited.

2 SERVES | 15 PREP | 30 COOK | 498 CALORIES

2 SMALL SWEET POTATOES, SKIN ON, DICED

185G CAN TUNA, DRAINED

½ RED ONION, FINELY CHOPPED

100G FROZEN PEAS, DEFROSTED

1 EGG, BEATEN

40G BREADCRUMBS

OLIVE OIL

SALT AND PEPPER

SALAD, TO SERVE

Place the sweet potato in a saucepan, cover with boiling water and simmer for about 10 minutes until tender.

Drain the sweet potato and mash in a bowl. Season with salt and pepper. The skin will be visible as brown flecks, which may not be pretty but will give you extra fibre, and we all need more of that in our diet.

Add the tuna, red onion and peas and mix together well. Stir in the beaten egg and mix well again.

Divide the tuna mixture into 4 and form each portion into a fish cake. Coat the fish cakes in the breadcrumbs, handling them gently.

Heat a little olive oil in a frying pan and fry the fish cakes for about 8 minutes on each side, turning frequently to get a uniform golden brown colour.

Serve the fish cakes with a side salad.

NUTRITION NUGGET
Sweet potatoes have a much lower glycaemic load than regular white potatoes, meaning they raise blood sugar more slowly.

RIVER COBBLER WITH BROAD BEAN MASH AND LIME ROCKET SALAD

River cobbler, sometimes called basa, is a cheap alternative to cod. It is equally as tasty and has the same type of texture, and can be used in just the same way.

1 SERVES
10 PREP
10 COOK
644 CALORIES

200G COOKED FROZEN OR DRAINED CANNED BROAD BEANS

40G FETA CHEESE

HANDFUL OF ROCKET

OLIVE OIL

JUICE OF ½ LIME

1 RIVER COBBLER (BASA) FILLET

SALT AND PEPPER

Place the broad beans in a bowl. Crumble in the feta cheese and add a little salt and pepper to taste, then mash roughly with a fork. Set aside.

Add the rocket to a small bowl and drizzle with a little olive oil and the lime juice. Toss together and set aside.

Heat a little olive oil in a frying pan and gently fry the river cobbler for about 3–4 minutes on each side. Season with a little salt and pepper.

Arrange the mash in the centre of a plate. Place the fish on top and finally garnish the fish with the rocket salad.

NUTRITION NUGGET
Broad beans are a great source of magnesium and fibre.

SALMON, RED PEPPER AND BLACK OLIVE STEW

Perfect any time of year, this gorgeous dish captures many of the typical Mediterranean flavours that we have all come to know and love. It's also a great way to introduce salmon to fussier eaters, because the dominant flavours here moderate the salmon taste a little. Skinless salmon fillets can be bought frozen, but otherwise ask the fishmonger to skin them for you, or see below for how to do it yourself. If cooking for fewer people, the surplus stew can be cooled and frozen as a whole or in individual portions, then defrosted before gently reheating for an ultra-easy option when you need it most.

4 SERVES | **15 PREP** | **25 COOK** | **409 CALORIES**

OLIVE OIL

1 LARGE RED ONION, FINELY CHOPPED

3 LARGE GARLIC CLOVES, FINELY CHOPPED

2 RED PEPPERS, CORED, DESEEDED AND DICED

4 SKINLESS SALMON FILLETS, DICED (OR SEE METHOD IF YOU WANT/NEED TO REMOVE THE SKIN YOURSELF)

400G CAN CHOPPED TOMATOES

2 TABLESPOONS PITTED BLACK OLIVES

2 TEASPOONS BRINE FROM THE OLIVES

SALT

BAKED SWEET POTATO, TO SERVE

If you want to skin the salmon fillets yourself, simply lay the fish flesh side down, take a corner and make a small cut just underneath the skin to separate the corner of skin from the flesh. Then turn the fish over and, starting at that corner, run the knife along the inside of the skin to cut it clean away from the flesh.

Heat a little olive oil in a saucepan, add the red onion, garlic and red peppers along with a generous pinch of salt and sauté until the onion has softened and the peppers are beginning to soften.

Add the diced salmon, canned tomatoes, olives and olive brine and simmer for about 15–20 minutes until the salmon is cooked, the peppers are soft and the flavour of the mixture has matured.

The stew is perfect served over a baked sweet potato.

NUTRITION NUGGET
Tomatoes are a great source of a carotenoid called lycopene that has reported benefits for prostate health.

FANCY FISH CURRY

This is an interesting fusion-type curry. Imagine the texture of the lentil-based Indian dishes dhansak or dhal crossed with the flavour profile of a Thai curry. That's what we have here, and it tastes out of this world.

4 SERVES **20 PREP** **35 COOK** **669 CALORIES**

2 LARGE LEMON GRASS STALKS

OLIVE OIL

1 LARGE RED ONION, FINELY CHOPPED

4 GARLIC CLOVES, FINELY CHOPPED

1 GREEN CHILLI, FINELY CHOPPED

250G DRIED RED LENTILS

400ML CAN COCONUT MILK

200–300ML VEGETABLE STOCK

2 SKINLESS SALMON FILLETS, DICED

2 SKINLESS COD FILLETS, DICED

2 HANDFULS OF BABY SPINACH

SALT

Take a rolling pin or suitable alternative heavy implement and give the lemon grass stalks a good wallop. This will bruise and split them, which allows their essential oils to be released and infuse the dish with their flavour.

Heat a little olive oil in a pan, add the red onion, garlic, lemon grass and chilli along with a good pinch of salt and sauté until the onion has softened and the lemon grass becomes fragrant.

Add the lentils and the coconut milk and simmer for 5–6 minutes, stirring frequently. Then add the stock in increments – think of it like making a risotto, adding it little and often and stirring frequently, until the dish resembles porridge in texture. If you run out of stock, you can use a little water to get you to this stage.

Once the dish has reached the required consistency, drop in the diced fish and simmer gently for a further 6–7 minutes until it is cooked, stirring frequently but gently so that the fish doesn't fall apart.

Throw in the baby spinach and stir until it has wilted before serving.

NUTRITION NUGGET
Pulses such as lentils are great sources of B vitamins and fibre, and have been shown to help lower cholesterol when consumed regularly.

SALMON BURGERS WITH CHILLI AIOLI

These gorgeous burgers are a great midweek treat. Weirdly, they don't taste very fishy at all, and end up very meaty, so it's a perfect dish for those who are timid about eating fish.

4 SERVES   **20** PREP   **10** COOK   **554** CALORIES

4 SKINLESS SALMON FILLETS

4 GARLIC CLOVES, FINELY CHOPPED, SEPARATED INTO 2 BATCHES

1 RED ONION, ½ FINELY CHOPPED, ½ SLICED INTO RINGS

SMALL BUNCH OF CORIANDER, ROUGHLY CHOPPED (OPTIONAL)

OLIVE OIL

2 TABLESPOONS MAYONNAISE

1 TEASPOON MEDIUM CHILLI POWDER

1 TEASPOON LEMON JUICE

4 WHOLEWHEAT OR MULTIGRAIN BUNS

HANDFUL OF BABY SPINACH

SALT AND PEPPER

Place the skinless salmon fillets in a food processor and blitz into an even mince-like texture.

Remove the blades from the processor. Add half the garlic, the finely chopped red onion and the coriander, if using, along with a good pinch of salt and pepper, and mix together well.

Divide the salmon mixture into 4 and use your hands to form each portion into a burger patty.

Heat a little olive oil in a frying pan and gently fry the burgers for about 4 minutes on each side, just long enough to turn them lightly golden brown.

Meanwhile, mix the mayo, remaining garlic, chilli powder and lemon juice together in a small bowl.

Slice the buns in half horizontally. Place a few baby spinach leaves and a couple of red onion rings on each bottom half. Sit a burger on top, then smother the burger with a generous dollop of the chilli aioli. Finish with the top half of each bun.

NUTRITION NUGGET
Using wholewheat or multigrain buns here means more fibre and B vitamins and a slower elevation of blood sugar, which helps you to stay feeling fuller for longer.

PIMPED-UP PAELLA

The reason this paella recipe is pimped up is pretty simple. It's not that I've made it insanely complex but I've upgraded the rice by swapping out white for brown. The result is more fibre and B vitamins, plus it keeps you feeling fuller for longer and also helps stabilize blood sugar – all from just one swap! Using the frozen seafood mix here saves you money, preparation time and fuss.

4 SERVES **10** PREP **40** COOK **447** CALORIES

OLIVE OIL

1 RED ONION, FINELY CHOPPED

3 GARLIC CLOVES, FINELY CHOPPED

300G BROWN RICE

1 TEASPOON SMOKED PAPRIKA

3 TABLESPOONS WHITE WINE

400G CAN CHOPPED TOMATOES

900ML FISH STOCK
(CHICKEN STOCK IS FINE TOO)

400G FROZEN SEAFOOD MIX

SALT

LEMON WEDGES AND COOKED
GREENS OR SALAD, TO SERVE

Heat a little olive oil in a large, deep frying pan, add the red onion and garlic along with good pinch of salt and sauté until the onion has softened.

Stir in the rice, paprika and white wine and simmer long enough for the liquid to evaporate.

Add the canned tomatoes and stock and simmer for about 20–25 minutes. You MUST stir regularly to prevent sticking, and brown rice can take a while to cook, so keep your eye on it!

Stir the seafood mix into the pan and simmer for a further 5–7 minutes.

Serve with the lemon wedges to squeeze over and either cooked greens or a salad.

NUTRITION NUGGET
Seafood is often shunned in this country, yet it's an incredibly rich source of nutrients, such as the mineral zinc. This performs hundreds of roles in the body, including keeping skin healthy, fighting infection and maintaining levels of key hormones.

CHILLI PRAWNS WITH RED ONION AND COURGETTES

This is a dead-easy dish that makes a speedy lunch or dinner when you want something fresh and tasty but don't want to wait an hour and a half for the pleasure.

4 SERVES · **15** PREP · **20** COOK · **111** CALORIES

OLIVE OIL

1 LARGE RED ONION, HALVED AND SLICED LENGTHWAYS

4 GARLIC CLOVES, ROUGHLY CHOPPED

2 COURGETTES, SLICED INTO BATONS

350G UNCOOKED PEELED KING PRAWNS

2 TEASPOONS CLEAR HONEY

½ TEASPOON SMOKED PAPRIKA

1 RED CHILLI, THINLY SLICED

SALT

NOODLES OR BROWN RICE, TO SERVE

Heat a little olive oil in a frying pan or wok, add the red onion and garlic along with a good pinch of salt and sauté until the onion is beginning to soften.

Add the courgettes and continue to cook until all the veg has softened, about 8 minutes.

Add the prawns and cook for 2–3 minutes, stirring continuously.

Add the honey, paprika and chilli and cook for a further 3–4 minutes until the flavours have concentrated.

Serve with noodles or brown rice.

NUTRITION NUGGET
Chillies contain a substance called capsaicin that gives them their powerful heat. Capsaicin can act as a decongestant and a painkiller, and can even stimulate circulation.

CHILLI AND LIME SALMON PARCELS

As simple as it gets, this is the ideal way to cook fish if you need a quick and healthy throw-together meal after a long day. You can concoct every conceivable flavour combination you fancy, and it keeps the prepping of ingredients to a minimum, not to mention saving on the washing-up!

 2 SERVES

 15 PREP

 25 COOK

357 CALORIES

2 SKINLESS SALMON FILLETS

2 GARLIC CLOVES, SLICED

1 GREEN CHILLI, SLICED

2CM PIECE OF FRESH ROOT GINGER, PEELED AND SLICED

JUICE OF 1 LIME

2 TEASPOONS SESAME OIL

BROWN RICE AND STIR-FRIED GREENS, TO SERVE

Preheat the oven to 190°C/170°C fan/Gas Mark 5.

Using sheets of foil, make 2 rectangular bowls that are big enough to house the salmon fillets, with sides high enough to hold all the other ingredients. Make sure they are watertight and that there are no holes. Place the foil bowls on a baking tray.

Add a salmon fillet to each foil bowl and then divide the remaining ingredients between the bowls so that they completely cover and bathe the fish.

Bake for 18–20 minutes until the flesh of the salmon flakes easily when prodded with a fork.

Serve the salmon with some brown rice and stir-fried greens, using the liquid in the foil bowl as the sauce to bathe all the accompaniments too.

NUTRITION NUGGET
Salmon really is a nutritional powerhouse. It's chock-full of vitamins and minerals, such as vitamins B12 and D and selenium. And let's not forget its exceptional omega-3 fatty acid content.

EASY KING PRAWN CURRY

Cooking curries from scratch can sometimes seem a little daunting. This one is a great introduction to curry making, as it really isn't complex at all yet it tastes sublime.

2-3 SERVES   **20** PREP   **30** COOK   **376** CALORIES

1 LARGE ONION, ROUGHLY CHOPPED

4 GARLIC CLOVES, FINELY CHOPPED

1 RED CHILLI, ROUGHLY CHOPPED

OLIVE OIL

2.5CM PIECE OF FRESH ROOT GINGER, PEELED AND ROUGHLY CHOPPED

200G CHERRY TOMATOES, CHOPPED

2 TEASPOONS MILD CURRY POWDER

1 TEASPOON GROUND TURMERIC

1 TEASPOON GROUND CORIANDER

1 TEASPOON GARAM MASALA

½ TEASPOON GROUND CUMIN

400G UNCOOKED PEELED KING PRAWNS

3 TABLESPOONS FULL-FAT NATURAL YOGURT

½ TEASPOON GROUND CINNAMON

HANDFUL OF CORIANDER LEAVES, ROUGHLY CHOPPED (OPTIONAL)

SALT

Place the onion, garlic and chilli in a food processor and blitz to create a fine purée.

Heat a little olive oil in a large saucepan, add the onion purée and chopped ginger along with a good pinch of salt and cook for 10 minutes, or until the purée is darker in colour and less pungent in taste and aroma. I always say, if you think it's done, give it another 7–8 minutes – it really is worth the extra time!

Once the purée reaches this stage, add the tomatoes and all the spices except the cinnamon. Cook for a further 10 minutes, stirring frequently.

Add the prawns and yogurt and cook for another 10 minutes, stirring frequently. Stir in the cinnamon and garnish with coriander, if you like.

NUTRITION NUGGET

Ginger contains an array of essential oils that give it its zingy flavour, and which are known to have anti-inflammatory properties. If you have a cold, a shot of fresh ginger is great for reducing the inflammation in the mucous membranes, helping you breathe more easily.

MAPLE MUSTARD SALMON WITH PAPRIKA SWEET POTATO WEDGES AND GREEN SALAD

Such a wonderful marriage of flavours, this dish is super filling and very straightforward to make.

2 SERVES | **15 PREP** | **30 COOK** | **882 CALORIES**

2 TABLESPOONS MAPLE SYRUP

2 TEASPOONS WHOLEGRAIN MUSTARD

2 TEASPOONS SESAME OIL

2 SKINLESS SALMON FILLETS

1 LARGE SWEET POTATO, SKIN ON, CUT INTO WEDGES

OLIVE OIL

1 TEASPOON SMOKED PAPRIKA

½ TEASPOON GARLIC SALT

2 HANDFULS OF BABY SPINACH

3 SPRING ONIONS, CUT INTO BATONS

2 HANDFULS OF SUGAR SNAP PEAS

FOR THE SALAD DRESSING

JUICE OF 1 LIME

1 TABLESPOON OLIVE OIL

1 TEASPOON SESAME OIL

Preheat the oven to 180°C/160°C fan/Gas Mark 4.

Mix the maple syrup, mustard and sesame oil together in a bowl to create a marinade. Add the salmon fillets and turn to coat in marinade, then set aside.

Place the sweet potato wedges on a baking tray, drizzle with a little olive oil and toss together well. Sprinkle the smoked paprika and garlic salt over the wedges and toss well again until coated.

Remove the salmon from the marinade and place on a lightly oiled baking tray. Bake along with the wedges for 25–30 minutes until the flesh of the fish flakes easily when prodded with a fork, removing the tray halfway through and spooning a little of the leftover marinade over the salmon before returning to the oven.

Meanwhile, toss the spinach, spring onions and sugar snap peas together in a bowl. Whisk the dressing ingredients together before using to dress the salad.

Once the salmon is baked and the sweet potato wedges are soft and golden brown at the edges, serve with the salad alongside.

NUTRITION NUGGET

All types of onion have wonderful benefits for digestive health. They contain something called inulin, which feeds the good bacteria that live in the gut, helping them to thrive as a colony.

SMOKED SALMON, AVOCADO AND WASABI STACK

This makes a great starter that's bursting with flavour and nutrition. It looks pretty funky too. Use two small ring moulds (about 7cm in diameter and 3.5cm deep) that come with a handy pusher to compact the ingredients and create a uniformly neat stack on each plate.

2 SERVES

15 PREP

548 CALORIES

2 AVOCADOS, STONED, PEELED AND DICED

200G SMOKED SALMON, CHOPPED

1 TABLESPOON MAYONNAISE

JUICE OF ½ LEMON

2 TEASPOONS WASABI PASTE

2 CORIANDER SPRIGS, TO GARNISH

Mix all the ingredients (except the garnish) together in a bowl until they are well combined.

Place a small ring mould on each serving plate. Divide the mixture between the 2 rings and use the pusher that comes with the moulds to press the ingredients down into the mould and compact them well. Lift off each ring in turn to reveal the moulded stack.

Garnish each stack with a coriander sprig.

NUTRITION NUGGET

The wasabi root, which belongs to the same plant family as horseradish and is sometimes called Japanese horseradish, was traditionally used medicinally to clear a chesty cough and act as a decongestant.

COD AND CHORIZO ONE POT

The Prawn and Chorizo Mash-up in the first *Eat Shop Save* book was incredibly popular, so I thought I would sneak another chorizo dish in here. Sure, I can't claim that chorizo is a health food, but if its inclusion makes the difference between someone eating a nutritious array of ingredients or not, then what the heck. This book is about making healthier food accessible, right?

4 SERVES · **15 PREP** · **25 COOK** · **477 CALORIES**

OLIVE OIL

1 RED ONION, FINELY CHOPPED

3 GARLIC CLOVES, FINELY CHOPPED

1 RED PEPPER, HALVED, CORED AND DESEEDED, THEN CUT INTO LONG BATONS

200G CHORIZO, CUT INTO SMALL DICE

400G CAN CHOPPED TOMATOES

400G CAN WHITE BEANS (CANNELLINI, BUTTER OR HARICOT), DRAINED

100ML WATER

4 SKINLESS COD FILLETS

SALT

LIGHTLY COOKED GREENS OR SALAD, TO SERVE

Heat a little olive oil in a wide pan, add the red onion, garlic and red pepper along with a good pinch of salt and sauté until the onion has softened.

Stir in the chorizo and cook for a further few minutes until the chorizo has turned the onion and garlic an orangey colour.

Add the canned tomatoes and beans and the measured water and simmer for 2–3 minutes until the pepper has fully softened and the sauce is beginning to thicken.

Gently place the cod fillets in the sauce, reduce the heat and simmer for about 10 minutes until lightly cooked.

Serve with some lightly cooked greens or a salad.

NUTRITION NUGGET
Cod is a great protein source and also a good source of the mineral selenium, which aids cellular repair.

PLANT BASED

CHAPTER
5

There is no escaping the fact that vegan food has become big news, with the UK witnessing an enormous rise in veganism. However, I have carefully chosen to use the term 'plant based' for this chapter rather than 'vegan' as I'm looking at a purely dietary approach, whereas veganism goes far beyond diet. It's a complete set of ethical values that governs many aspects of a person's life, from the clothes they wear to the cosmetics they use as well as the food they eat.

A plant-based diet undoubtedly offers health benefits, especially for those schooled in the typical UK diet, as it's incredibly high in fibre, vitamins, minerals, antioxidants and phytochemicals. It also has the POTENTIAL (chips and tofu nuggets, for instance, are vegan, but health food they are not) to be low in many of the damaging substances that are found in our modern processed diets. Plus it can greatly enhance cardiovascular health, and is often associated with improved body composition too. I myself was vegan for over 20 years – although I am no longer, which is a conversation for another day – yet I can still testify to the many possible benefits of this way of eating. It does, however, have some potential downfalls, as there are a few key nutrients missing from a plant-based diet – vitamin B12 in particular, which is essential for red blood cell formation. But if you are aware of these deficiencies and take the right remedial action, it's a healthy diet that can be followed for life.

THE EAT SHOP SAV£ WAY

Vegetable risotto in a restaurant =
700 calories per serving
27g fat

Sun-dried Tomato, Courgette and Red
Pepper Risotto (page 126) =
525 calories per serving
8g fat

Additional benefits include:
» Over 100% of our recommended daily intake of vitamin A
» Over 100% of our recommended daily intake of vitamin C

NUTRITION NUGGET

The process that produces brown rice removes only the outermost layer,
the hull, of the rice kernel and is the least damaging to its nutritional value.
The complete milling and polishing that converts brown rice into white rice
can destroy up to 60% of the vitamin B3, 80% of the vitamin B1, 90% of the
vitamin B6, half of the manganese, half of the phosphorus, 60% of the iron, and
all of the dietary fibre and essential fatty acids.

Brown rice is an excellent source of manganese, which helps produce energy
from protein and carbohydrates and is involved in the synthesis of fatty acids,
which are important for a healthy nervous system, and in the production of
cholesterol, which is used by the body to produce sex hormones. Manganese
is also a critical component of a very important antioxidant enzyme called
superoxide dismutase. SOD is found inside the body's mitochondria (the
energy factories inside most of our cells) where it provides protection against
damage from the free radicals produced during energy production.

So as you can see, this simple swap from white rice to brown rice can make a
huge difference!

RED LENTIL, WHITE BEAN AND BUTTERNUT SQUASH STEW

Perfect as a warming winter dish, this recipe gives you a bowl
full of feel-good factor. It's simple one-pot cooking at its absolute
best, and an ideal candidate for doubling up the quantities
and freezing for an effortless meal at a later date.

2-3 SERVES | **15 PREP** | **25 COOK** | **513 CALORIES**

OLIVE OIL

1 RED ONION, FINELY CHOPPED

2 GARLIC CLOVES, FINELY CHOPPED

½ SMALL BUTTERNUT SQUASH,
SKIN ON, DESEEDED AND DICED

100–110G DRIED RED LENTILS

ABOUT 500ML VEGETABLE STOCK

400G CAN BUTTER BEANS, DRAINED

HANDFUL OF BABY SPINACH

SALT

Heat a little olive oil in a saucepan, add the red onion
and garlic along with a good pinch of salt and sauté
until the onion has softened.

Add the squash and lentils, then pour in enough
vegetable stock to almost cover everything – you may
not need all the stock, and if you need extra liquid, just
use a little water.

Simmer for about 20 minutes until the lentils have
almost completely broken down and created a thick
stew, and the squash is tender.

Add the butter beans and spinach together with a little
water if needed, and stir just until the spinach wilts
before serving.

NUTRITION NUGGET

The bright orange colour of butternut squash comes from
a substance called beta carotene. When we eat squash,
beta carotene can accumulate in the fatty subcutaneous
layer of our skin and protect structural proteins such
as collagen and elastin from damage. Leaving the skins
on the butternut squash will increase the fibre content
of this dish, helping to keep you feeling full for longer,
stabilize blood sugar and support digestive health
and gut bacteria.

SWEET POTATO AND CHICKPEA BAKE

This is such a lovely comforting dish, bursting with flavour
and packed with heart-healthy nutrients.

4 SERVES

20 PREP

35 COOK

571 CALORIES

2 LARGE SWEET POTATOES,
SKIN ON, DICED

OLIVE OIL

1 RED ONION, FINELY CHOPPED

1 GARLIC CLOVE, FINELY CHOPPED

2 HANDFULS OF BABY SPINACH

400G CAN CHICKPEAS, DRAINED

4 TABLESPOONS SUN-DRIED
TOMATO PASTE

SALT

Preheat the oven to 200°C/180°C fan/Gas Mark 6.

Place the diced sweet potato in a saucepan, cover
with boiling water and simmer for about 15 minutes
until tender.

Meanwhile, heat a little olive oil in a frying pan, add
the red onion and garlic along with a good pinch of salt
and sauté until the onion has softened.

Add the spinach and sauté until it has wilted.

Stir in the chickpeas, then add the sun-dried tomato
paste and mix together well.

Once the sweet potato is done, drain, return to the pan
and mash into a creamy orange mash.

Tip the chickpea mixture into a baking dish and spread
out into an even layer. Top with the mash, as you would
for a shepherd's pie. Bake for 15–20 minutes until the
mash has started to turn crispy.

NUTRITION NUGGET
Chickpeas are packed with B vitamins and zinc,
and are a great source of protein and fibre. Onions
and garlic help support digestion by feeding
the good bacteria that live in the digestive tract.

COURGETTE, CANNELLINI, COCONUT AND TOMATO STEW

Another beautiful one-pot dish, this is a fabulous fusion of different types of flavour. It's perfectly satisfying on its own, but you could serve it with some cooked greens or a salad.

2 SERVES

15 PREP

20 COOK

482 CALORIES

1 TABLESPOON OLIVE OIL

1 RED ONION, FINELY CHOPPED

2 GARLIC CLOVES, FINELY CHOPPED

1 SMALL COURGETTE, SLICED INTO ROUNDS

200G CANNED CHOPPED TOMATOES

200ML COCONUT MILK

400G CAN CANNELLINI BEANS, DRAINED

HANDFUL OF BABY SPINACH

SALT

Heat the olive oil in a saucepan, add the red onion, garlic and courgette along with a good pinch of salt and sauté until the onion has softened.

Add the canned tomatoes and coconut milk and simmer for about 10 minutes until the sauce reduces and thickens, stirring well throughout.

Stir in the cannellini beans and simmer for a further 5 minutes.

Add the baby spinach and stir just until it wilts before serving.

NUTRITION NUGGET

Don't be scared of fats: always opt for full-fat coconut milk. Natural unprocessed fats will keep you feeling full, help you to absorb fat-soluble nutrients like vitamin D and carotenoids and provide key fatty acids that support many aspects of our health.

NUTTY NOODLES

This recipe could have quite easily gone into the Bowl Food section of the book, but it's such a shining example of how delicious vegan/plant-based food can be that I just had to put it in here. A sure-fire candidate for a future food addiction!

1 SERVES

15 PREP

12 COOK

683 CALORIES

50G DRIED FLAT RICE NOODLES

COCONUT OIL OR OLIVE OIL

½ RED ONION, SLICED

2 GARLIC CLOVES, FINELY CHOPPED

1 SMALL RED CHILLI, FINELY CHOPPED

5–6 SHIITAKE MUSHROOMS, SLICED

1 HEAPED TABLESPOON CRUNCHY PEANUT BUTTER

2 TEASPOONS SOY SAUCE

½ TEASPOON CLEAR HONEY

150ML WATER

6–8 DICED PIECES OF FIRM TOFU

SALT

Place the rice noodles in a heatproof bowl, cover with boiling water and leave to soak for about 10 minutes until softened.

Meanwhile, heat a little coconut oil or olive oil in a large frying pan or wok, add the red onion, garlic and chilli along with a pinch of salt and sauté until the onion has almost softened.

Add the shiitake mushrooms and continue to sauté until these have softened.

Stir in the peanut butter, soy sauce, honey and measured water. Simmer for a few minutes until the sauce thickens, adding a little more water if needed to get the consistency of sauce you prefer.

Add the tofu to the sauce, then drain the rice noodles and add these too, tossing well while still on the heat to coat and combine before serving.

NUTRITION NUGGET
Peanut butter is often viewed as being unhealthy. Sure, it contains a lot of calories (although we now know they aren't the be all and end all), but it's a great source of B vitamins, zinc and magnesium. Just keep away from the nasty highly processed versions that are full of sugar and dodgy oils.

BANGIN' BEAN BURGER

Ok, so bean burgers may have a bit of a reputation as being a dull, boring, unimaginative addition to a plant-based menu or the stereotypical vegetarian option. However, they can be absolutely gorgeous, as I hope this recipe will prove. If you want to make extra to freeze, or you only want one or two burgers, lay the uncooked patties on a baking sheet and place in the freezer for a few hours until frozen, then transfer to a ziplock bag or sealed container. Defrost and then cook as per the recipe.

4 SERVES
15 PREP
20 COOK
349 CALORIES

2 X 400G CANS MIXED BEANS, DRAINED

150G WHOLEMEAL BREADCRUMBS

½ RED ONION, FINELY CHOPPED

2 GARLIC CLOVES, FINELY CHOPPED

3 TEASPOONS MADRAS CURRY PASTE

LARGE BUNCH OF CORIANDER, ROUGHLY CHOPPED

SALT

WHOLEMEAL BUNS, LETTUCE, SLICED TOMATO AND SLICED RED ONION, TO SERVE

Tip the mixed beans into a bowl and mash them with a fork until almost completely broken down to a paste-like texture.

Add all the remaining ingredients, season with salt and mix together well.

Preheat the grill and line a baking tray with foil.

Divide the bean mixture into 4 and form each portion into a burger patty. Carefully lay them on the foil-lined tray and place under the grill for about 15–20 minutes, turning frequently but gently, until golden and crisp.

Serve in wholemeal buns with lettuce, sliced tomato and sliced onion.

NUTRITION NUGGET
The well-known side effect associated with eating beans is usually only temporary. It arises from our gut bacteria breaking down large sugar molecules found in the beans, a by-product of which is gas. However, this process encourages the bacterial colony in the gut to grow and flourish.

SUN-DRIED TOMATO, COURGETTE AND RED PEPPER RISOTTO

I've pimped up the classic risotto here, nutritionally speaking, by swapping the usual short-grain white rice for brown.

4 SERVES   **15** PREP   **45** COOK   **525** CALORIES

OLIVE OIL

2 LARGE RED ONIONS, FINELY CHOPPED

4 GARLIC CLOVES, FINELY CHOPPED

120G DRAINED SUN-DRIED TOMATOES IN OIL, HALVED

500G SHORT-GRAIN BROWN RICE

800G CANNED CHOPPED TOMATOES

2 LITRES VEGETABLE STOCK

2 COURGETTES, SLICED

2 RED PEPPERS, CORED, DESEEDED AND DICED

SALT

Heat a little olive oil in a large saucepan, add the red onion, garlic and sun-dried tomatoes along with a good pinch of salt and sauté until the onion has softened.

Add the rice and canned tomatoes and simmer until the liquid has reduced, stirring frequently.

Start adding the vegetable stock little and often, simmering and stirring frequently until each addition is absorbed before adding the next.

When the rice is about two-thirds of the way cooked, i.e. when you bite into a grain, it's soft on the outside but still crunchy on the inside, stir in the courgettes and red peppers (adding them earlier will make them way too overcooked).

Continue adding the stock bit by bit until it has all been absorbed, the rice is fully cooked and the consistency of the dish is reminiscent of a thick porridge. The rice will take about 35 minutes to cook in total.

NUTRITION NUGGET
One-pot cooking is a great way to retain water-soluble nutrients such as B vitamins. Boiling vegetables, for example, can result in the cooking water containing more nutrients than the veg that you're going to eat! But when everything is cooked in one pot, you can be sure that no goodness is lost.

ROASTED ROOTS WITH CREAMY WHITE BEAN PURÉE

This is such a beautiful and filling dish. As well as having a wonderfully satisfying texture contrast, it has an amazing nutritional profile.

2 SERVES | 20 PREP | 35 COOK | 499 CALORIES

2 PARSNIPS, SKIN ON,
CUT INTO THICK BATONS

2 CARROTS, SKIN ON,
CUT INTO THICK BATONS

2 BEETROOT, SKIN ON,
CUT INTO WEDGES

1 RED ONION, CUT INTO WEDGES

OLIVE OIL

1 TEASPOON DRIED MIXED HERBS

¼ TEASPOON GROUND CUMIN

¼ TEASPOON GROUND CINNAMON

400G CAN CANNELLINI BEANS,
DRAINED

1 TABLESPOON TAHINI

JUICE OF 1 LEMON

1 LARGE GARLIC CLOVE,
FINELY CHOPPED

SALT AND PEPPER

Preheat the oven to 180°C/160°C fan/Gas Mark 4.

Place the parsnips, carrots, beetroot and red onion in a roasting tin. Drizzle with olive oil and toss together well. Sprinkle over the mixed herbs, cumin and cinnamon along with a good pinch of salt and pepper and mix well again.

Roast the veg for 30–35 minutes, turning occasionally.

Meanwhile, place the cannellini beans, tahini, lemon juice, garlic and a good pinch of salt in a food processor or blender and blitz into a smooth purée.

To serve, place a generous dollop of the white bean purée in the centre of each serving plate, then smear it out in a circle with the back of the spoon to cover a larger surface area of the plate. Heap the roasted roots on top, then drizzle over any cooking juices left in the roasting tin.

NUTRITION NUGGET
Beetroot contains substances called nitrates that convert into something called nitric oxide in the body. Nitric oxide widens blood vessels and improves circulation to the extremities. This can enhance athletic performance and lower blood pressure.

HUMMUS, ROASTED ONION AND RAINBOW SLAW WRAP

This wrap makes the perfect portable work lunch, and the recipe will give you enough of the three different delicious filling elements to make three days' worth in advance.

3 SERVES **15** PREP **30** COOK **533** CALORIES

2 RED ONIONS, HALVED AND SLICED LENGTHWAYS

400G CAN CHICKPEAS, DRAINED

2 TABLESPOONS TAHINI

JUICE OF 1 LARGE LEMON

1 LARGE GARLIC CLOVE, FINELY CHOPPED

¼ RED CABBAGE, FINELY SHREDDED

1 SMALL CARROT, FINELY SHREDDED

1 TABLESPOON COCONUT YOGURT (OPTIONAL)

1 WHOLEMEAL WRAP OR TORTILLA PER SERVING

SALT

Begin by roasting the onions. Preheat the oven to 180°C/160°C fan/Gas Mark 4.

Place the red onion slices on a baking tray and bake for 25–30 minutes until soft and just beginning to turn golden brown at the edges.

To make the hummus, place the chickpeas, tahini, lemon juice and garlic in a food processor or blender and blitz until smooth. Season to taste with salt.

To make the slaw, place the cabbage, carrot and coconut yogurt, if using, along with a good pinch of salt in a bowl and toss together well.

Lay a wrap out flat. Arrange one-third of the slaw in a line through the centre. Top with one-third of the roasted onions, then top it all off with one-third of the hummus. Wrap up tightly.

The leftover fillings can be stored in separate sealed containers in the fridge for 3–4 days.

NUTRITION NUGGET
Wraps are the ideal healthier alternative to regular sandwiches. You get the same hand-held convenience but with a lower glycaemic load due to the less-starchy bread.

SPEEDY CHICKPEA AND SPINACH CURRY

Simple yet flavoursome, this is a great dish for when you really can't be bothered to spend ages in the kitchen, but want something decent. Winner, winner chickpea dinner!

2 SERVES **10** PREP **20** COOK **762** CALORIES

OLIVE OIL

1 LARGE RED ONION, FINELY CHOPPED

3 GARLIC CLOVES, FINELY CHOPPED

2 TABLESPOONS CURRY PASTE (HOW HOT IS UP TO YOU)

400G CAN CHOPPED TOMATOES

2 X 400G CANS CHICKPEAS, DRAINED

250G BABY SPINACH

SALT

BROWN RICE, TO SERVE

Heat a little olive oil in a saucepan, add the red onion and garlic along with a good pinch of salt and sauté until the onion starts to soften.

Add in the curry paste and cook, stirring, for a further 2–3 minutes.

Add the canned tomatoes and simmer for 7–8 minutes until the sauce reduces.

Tip in the chickpeas and simmer. stirring occasionally, for another 2–3 minutes.

Add the baby spinach and stir just until wilted before serving.

Serve with brown rice.

NUTRITION NUGGET

Many of the spices commonly used in curries contain incredibly complex chemistry that can have valuable medicinal effects, including anti-inflammatory and antioxidant properties, enhancing circulation, acting as a decongestant and supporting digestion.

CAULIFLOWER 'STEAK' WITH BALSAMIC ROOT ROAST

Who would have thought it...cauliflower steak has become 'a thing'!

1 SERVES | 20 PREP | 40 COOK | 353 CALORIES

½ SMALL BEETROOT, SKIN ON, CUT INTO WEDGES

1 LARGE CARROT, CUT INTO LARGE BATONS

OLIVE OIL

2 TEASPOONS BALSAMIC VINEGAR

½ TEASPOON SMOKED PAPRIKA

½ TEASPOON GARLIC SALT

¼ TEASPOON GROUND CUMIN

1 THICK SLICE OF CAULIFLOWER, CUT LENGTHWAYS THROUGH THE CENTRE

LARGE HANDFUL OF SHREDDED SPRING GREENS

SALT

Preheat the oven to 180°C/160°C fan/Gas Mark 4. Begin by roasting the roots. Place the beetroot and carrot on a baking tray, drizzle with a little olive oil and sprinkle with a pinch of salt, then toss together well. Roast for 35–40 minutes, removing the tray halfway through, drizzling with the balsamic vinegar and tossing well again before returning to the oven.

Meanwhile, place 1 tablespoon of olive oil, the smoked paprika, garlic salt and cumin in a small bowl and whisk together well with a fork.

Place the cauliflower slice on another baking tray, pour over the oil and spice mixture and turn the cauli slice over a few times to completely coat it in the mix. Roast the cauliflower slice along with the roasting roots for 15–20 minutes until soft and golden brown.

Meanwhile, place the spring greens in a steamer or, if you don't have one, a metal sieve or colander set over a saucepan of boiling water and covered with a lid. Steam for 10 minutes until tender and bright green.

Serve the roasted cauli 'steak' and roots with the vibrant spring greens alongside.

NUTRITION NUGGET
As with all the cruciferous vegetables, cauliflower is very rich in a group of substances called glucosinolates that can activate cellular repair mechanisms, keeping our cells and, more importantly, our DNA protected against damage. Glucosinolates also help to stimulate detoxification in the liver.

IMAM BAYILDI

The name of this classic Turkish recipe translates as 'the imam fainted', due to the overwhelming deliciousness of the dish, so the legend goes!

2 SERVES
15 PREP
40 COOK
213 CALORIES

2 AUBERGINES

OLIVE OIL

1 LARGE RED ONION, FINELY CHOPPED

3 GARLIC CLOVES, FINELY CHOPPED

400G CAN CHOPPED TOMATOES

2 TEASPOONS GROUND CINNAMON

1 TEASPOON CLEAR HONEY

SALT

SALAD, TO SERVE

Preheat the oven to 180°C/160°C fan/Gas Mark 4.

Halve the aubergines lengthways and place them cut side up on a baking tray. Score the flesh in a crisscross pattern. Drizzle with a little olive oil and season with salt. Bake for 20 minutes until soft.

Meanwhile, make the stuffing. Heat a little olive oil in a pan, add the red onion and garlic along with a good pinch of salt and sauté until the onion has softened.

Add the canned tomatoes, cinnamon, honey and a pinch of salt and simmer for 15 minutes until the sauce has thickened and intensified.

Remove the aubergines from the oven and carefully scoop out the flesh, leaving the skins intact. Roughly chop the flesh and stir it into the tomato mixture until well combined.

Spoon the aubergine and tomato mixture into the aubergine skins and return to the oven to bake for 20 minutes.

Serve with a good hearty salad.

NUTRITION NUGGET
Aubergines contain a purple colour pigment called nasunin that has been shown to protect nerve cell membranes from damage.

BLACK BEAN CHILLI

This is a gorgeous, sumptuous plant-based version of a chilli.
Cans of black beans are now easy to find, available in almost every
supermarket. A good dish to keep on standby in the freezer.

4 SERVES

10 PREP

35 COOK

359 CALORIES

OLIVE OIL

2 RED ONIONS, FINELY CHOPPED

4 GARLIC CLOVES, FINELY CHOPPED

2 X 400G CANS CHOPPED TOMATOES

2 X 400G CANS BLACK BEANS, DRAINED

3 TEASPOONS SMOKED PAPRIKA

3 TEASPOONS GROUND CUMIN

SALT

CORIANDER LEAVES, TO GARNISH

BROWN RICE AND NATURAL YOGURT, TO SERVE

Heat a little olive oil in a pan, add the red onions and garlic along with a good pinch of salt and sauté until the onions have softened.

Add all the remaining ingredients and simmer gently for 30 minutes, stirring frequently. The chilli will thicken and the flavours intensify.

Garnish with some fresh coriander leaves and serve with brown rice and a dollop of yogurt.

NUTRITION NUGGET
Black beans are actually a very dark, intense purple. The colour pigment comes from a group of chemicals called anthocyanins that can lower blood pressure and protect blood vessels from damage.

BOWL
FOOD

CHAPTER

6

There is something innately comforting about bowl food, whether it's a nice steaming bowl of pasta in a rich flavoursome sauce, noodles in a warming soup or the new craze of Buddha bowls. Bowls are a great opportunity to combine all manner of healthy ingredients, are usually quick and easy to make and can be some of the most enjoyable meals imaginable. These dishes won't disappoint.

The other beauty about bowls is that if you have prepped ahead, they can be real time-savers too. Take the Salmon and Avocado Rice Bowl on page 164. A lot of these ingredients can be prepared a couple of days beforehand and then kept in the fridge, so this would make the perfect throw-together lunch. Keeping staples on hand such as quinoa, chicken breast and cooked fish means that you can devise a wide range of bowl concoctions with very little time and effort. Get creative and see what happens.

THE EAT SHOP SAV£ WAY

Ham and mushroom tagliatelle
ready meal =
700 calories per portion
8.3g fat
2.3g salt

Chicken Tagliatelle with Roasted
Red Pepper Sauce (page 158) =
600 calories per serving
2.7g fat
1.3g salt

Additional benefits include:
» 35% of our recommended daily intake of zinc
» Over 100% of our recommended daily intake of B1 and B3
» 300% of our recommended daily intake vitamin C!

NUTRITION NUGGET

Making your own pasta sauce from scratch is not only a doddle but it means you can control exactly what goes into it. Ready meals from the supermarket often contain a lot of salt and preservatives. My beautiful chicken tagliatelle is not only much lower in salt than a shop-bought version, but it also contains some important nutrients that a supermarket version is likely to be devoid of.

Peppers are packed with vitamins and minerals. They are an excellent source of vitamin C, vitamin A (in the form of carotenoids) and vitamin B6. In fact, peppers have one of the highest contents of vitamin C of all fruits and vegetables. They also provide us with a good number of B vitamins (including vitamin B2, B3, folate and B5, as well as vitamin E, potassium and molybdenum. Peppers also contain vitamin K, vitamin B1, manganese, phosphorus and magnesium in good amounts. As you can see, we get a wealth of nutrients from this brightly coloured vegetable. So make sure you pick up a pepper!

BREAKFAST SMOOTHIE BOWL

Smoothie bowls have become a highly fashionable item in recent times.
They are a convenient way to pack in lots of antioxidant-rich fruit,
but the downside of smoothies is that they can spike blood sugar rapidly.
So I have included a protein powder here to slow down the release
of the sugars in the fruit. Adding some yogurt will do the same job.

1 SERVES **10 PREP** **612 CALORIES**

1 BANANA, PEELED AND
BROKEN INTO PIECES

3 HANDFULS OF FROZEN
MIXED BERRIES

1 SCOOP OF VANILLA
PROTEIN POWDER

125ML MILK

TO DECORATE

1 TABLESPOON BLUEBERRIES

1 TABLESPOON SLICED STRAWBERRIES

Place the banana, frozen berries, protein powder and
milk in a blender and blend into a rich smoothie.

Pour into a bowl and decorate with the blueberries
and strawberry slices.

NUTRITION NUGGET
The deep purple colour in blueberries is produced
by compounds called flavonoids, which improve
many aspects of cardiovascular health, including
reducing blood pressure and increasing
resilience to vascular damage.

RAMEN BOWL

I have been lucky enough to spend a great deal of time in Japan, and one of the first things I do when I visit is head for a ramen shop. These wonderful noodles can be found floating around in a variety of delicious soups ranging from miso to pork broth, and everything in between. You really can throw any combination of ingredients into these.

1 SERVES

10 PREP

35 COOK

591 CALORIES

1 EGG

1 SKINLESS CHICKEN BREAST

85G DRIED RAMEN OR SOBA NOODLES

5–6 SHIITAKE MUSHROOMS (ABOUT 50G)

400ML WATER

2 TEASPOONS MISO PASTE

2 HANDFULS OF BABY SPINACH

Preheat the oven to 180°C/160°C fan/Gas Mark 4.

While the oven is heating up, bring a small saucepan of water to the boil, carefully lower the egg in and boil for 10 minutes until hard-boiled. Drain and run under cold water until cool enough to handle. Shell and leave to cool.

Place the chicken breast on a baking tray and bake for 20–25 minutes until cooked through.

Meanwhile, place the noodles in a saucepan, cover with boiling water and simmer for 5–7 minutes, or according to the packet instructions – just long enough for the noodles to soften. Drain and tip into a serving bowl.

Place the shiitake mushrooms in a saucepan and pour over the measured water. Bring to a gentle simmer and cook for 6–7 minutes until tender. Stir in the miso paste until dissolved.

Top the cooked noodles with the baby spinach, then pour over the miso broth and mushrooms. Cut the boiled egg in half lengthways, slice the chicken breast into bite-sized pieces and add both on top.

NUTRITION NUGGET
Miso is a rich source of plant chemicals called isoflavones. These have numerous health benefits, particularly in relation to hormone-related issues, with many claims that in higher doses they can help the prevention of hot flushes and other symptoms of the menopause.

GREEN PASTA

This pasta looks, well, a bit weird at first, but man alive, the flavour! In reality you can use almost anything in the sauce to enhance the taste, but these ingredients keep to the classic Italian flavour profile. Having said that, anything goes in cooking these days, so feel free to get adventurous.

2 SERVES

15 PREP

10 COOK

547 CALORIES

150G DRIED WHOLEWHEAT FUSILLI

OLIVE OIL

1 ONION, FINELY CHOPPED

3 GARLIC CLOVES, FINELY CHOPPED

4–5 HANDFULS OF FROZEN PEAS

30G BASIL

30G FLAT LEAF PARSLEY

100ML VEGETABLE STOCK

1 LARGE COURGETTE, CUT INTO ROUNDS

100ML SINGLE CREAM

SALT

Place the pasta in a large saucepan, cover with boiling water and simmer for 8–10 minutes, or according to the packet instructions, until al dente (cooked but slightly firm). When ready, drain and set aside.

While the pasta is cooking, heat a little olive oil in a saucepan, add the onion and garlic along with a good pinch of salt and sauté until the onion has softened.

Add the frozen peas, fresh herbs and stock, and simmer gently for a few minutes until the peas are soft.

While the peas are simmering, heat a little olive oil in a frying pan, add the courgette and sauté until softened.

Add the cream to the pea mixture and using a stick blender, or transferring to a regular blender, blitz into a smooth, vivid green sauce. If it's too thick, you can thin it down with a little water, added in tiny increments.

Add the cooked pasta to the sautéed courgette and mix together well. Pour over the green sauce and mix well again before dividing between 2 serving bowls.

NUTRITION NUGGET
Fresh herbs may seem like very basic ingredients, but they are often incredibly rich in powerful antioxidants and beneficial chemicals, many of which come from the chemistry responsible for their distinctive flavours. Basil has some very complex chemistry that produces its distinctive vibrant flavour. These substances offer potent antioxidant and anti-inflammatory activity.

GREEN CURRY NOODLES

Something I fell in love with from an early age was a dish called kari laksa,
which is a spicy coconut curry noodle soup hailing from Malaysia. In recent years
many other hybrids have started popping up, and the big noodle bar chains in the UK
have their versions of this classic. Using a green curry as a base for the noodles
works like a charm and green curry paste is easy to come by.

85G DRIED FLAT RICE NOODLES

OLIVE OIL

½ RED ONION, SLICED

2 GARLIC CLOVES, FINELY CHOPPED

2-3 HEAPED TEASPOONS
THAI GREEN CURRY PASTE

200ML COCONUT MILK

200ML VEGETABLE STOCK

70G UNCOOKED PEELED PRAWNS

70G UNCOOKED SQUID RINGS

½ COURGETTE, CUT INTO BATONS

4-5 CHESTNUT MUSHROOMS, SLICED

SALT

FRESH CORIANDER LEAVES,
TO GARNISH

Place the rice noodles in a heatproof bowl, cover with
boiling water and leave to soak for about 10 minutes
until softened. Drain and tip into a serving bowl.

While the noodles are soaking, heat a little olive oil in
a saucepan, add the onion and garlic along with a good
pinch of salt and sauté until the onion has softened.

Add all the remaining ingredients and simmer gently
for 10 minutes until everything is cooked.

Top the cooked noodles with the green seafood curry
and garnish with fresh coriander, if using.

NUTRITION NUGGET
Shellfish are a great source of the minerals zinc
and selenium, along with reasonable amounts
of omega-3 fatty acids.

VEGGIE-PACKED PENNE WITH FETA

This is one of my absolute favourite comfort foods. If it's freezing cold outside or if I'm feeling a bit down in the dumps, a bowl of this is the best tonic. There is just something so soothing about it, and it's packed with the good stuff too! Sun-dried tomato paste is now easy to find in jars in most supermarkets.

2 SERVES · **10 PREP** · **12 COOK** · **846 CALORIES**

- 150G DRIED WHOLEWHEAT PENNE
- OLIVE OIL
- 1 LARGE RED ONION, HALVED AND SLICED LENGTHWAYS
- 1 LARGE COURGETTE, CUT INTO HALF-ROUNDS
- 4–5 HANDFULS OF BABY SPINACH
- 75G SUN-DRIED TOMATO PASTE
- 60G FETA CHEESE
- SALT

Place the pasta in a large saucepan, cover with boiling water and simmer for about 10 minutes, or according to the packet instructions, until al dente (cooked but slightly firm). When ready, drain, reserving a splash of the cooking water, and set aside.

While the pasta is cooking, heat a little olive oil in a large frying pan, add the red onion along with a good pinch of salt and sauté until it has softened.

Add the courgette and continue to sauté for a few minutes until that has softened too. Add the baby spinach and sauté until it has wilted.

Stir the cooked pasta into the sautéed vegetables, making sure they are well combined.

Add the reserved water and then the sun-dried tomato paste in 2 batches, mixing well between each batch.

Divide the pasta between 2 serving bowls, then crumble the feta over each before serving.

NUTRITION NUGGET
Wholewheat pasta has a far lower glycaemic response than white pasta, meaning it doesn't cause blood sugar peaks and troughs. The higher fibre content also makes it beneficial for digestive and cardiovascular health.

ALL-IN-ONE EGG FRIED RICE

I use the term egg fried rice here in the very loosest of senses.
The egg is the thing that brings the dish together and provides a large
proportion of the protein hit. This really is a meal in itself, but
you could use it as a filling side dish.

2 SERVES | 15 PREP | 45 COOK | 722 CALORIES

150G BROWN RICE

OLIVE OIL

1 LARGE RED ONION, FINELY CHOPPED

4 GARLIC CLOVES, FINELY CHOPPED

2 SMALL CARROTS, DICED

2 HANDFULS OF CURLY KALE

4–5 SHIITAKE MUSHROOMS, SLICED

150G FIRM TOFU, CUBED

3 TEASPOONS SOY SAUCE

2 TEASPOONS TOASTED SESAME OIL

3 EGGS, BEATEN

SALT

Place the brown rice in a saucepan, cover with boiling water and simmer for about 30–40 minutes until tender and fluffy.

About halfway through the rice cooking time, heat a little olive oil in a large frying pan, add the red onion and garlic along with a good pinch of salt and sauté until the onion has softened.

Add the carrots and cook for a further 2–3 minutes. Then add the kale, mushrooms and tofu and cook for another 3–5 minutes.

When the rice is ready, drain and add to the vegetable mixture. Mix together well.

Add the soy sauce and sesame oil and mix in thoroughly.

Add the beaten eggs and stir occasionally until the egg is cooked through.

Divide the rice between 2 serving bowls.

NUTRITION NUGGET
Brown rice contains a substance called gamma oryzanol that has antioxidant properties and can lower cholesterol.

PAD THAI UPGRADED

I do love a good pad Thai, but it can often be swimming in refined sugar, and have little vegetable content beyond a tickle with a couple of bean sprouts. I have had some far more adventurous versions in Thailand, and with a bit of pimping up it can be a healthy light meal. You can swap the prawns for tofu and it works just as well.

1 SERVES   **15** PREP   **15** COOK   **592** CALORIES

OLIVE OIL

½ RED ONION, THINLY SLICED

1 GARLIC CLOVE, FINELY CHOPPED

1 GREEN CHILLI, THINLY SLICED

3–4 SPRING ONIONS, CUT INTO STRIPS

140G UNCOOKED PEELED KING PRAWNS

LARGE HANDFUL OF BABY SPINACH

75G DRIED FLAT RICE NOODLES

1 TEASPOON CLEAR HONEY

2 TEASPOONS FISH SAUCE OR SOY SAUCE

JUICE OF ½ LIME

1 EGG

1 TABLESPOON PEANUTS, ROUGHLY CRUSHED WITH THE BACK OF A SPOON

SALT

Heat a little olive oil in a large frying pan or wok, add the red onion, garlic and half the chilli along with a good pinch of salt and sauté until the onion has softened.

Throw in the spring onions and the prawns and continue to cook for 2–3 minutes until the spring onions soften a little. Add the baby spinach and sauté for a further minute or two until it has wilted and the prawns have turned pink.

Meanwhile, place the noodles in a heatproof bowl, cover with boiling water and leave to stand for about 10 minutes until partially but not fully softened.

Drain the noodles and add to the prawn mixture, where they will finish softening. Mix everything together well. Add the honey, fish or soy sauce and lime juice and toss together well.

Heat a little oil in a small pan, crack the egg into it and whisk it roughly with a fork. Leave the egg to cook until beginning to set, then stir and quickly scramble it. Stir the scrambled egg through the noodles.

Serve in a bowl, sprinkled with the roughly crushed peanuts and reserved chilli.

NUTRITION NUGGET
The substance that makes prawns pink is a carotenoid called astaxanthin that has health benefits for the eyes and the cardiovascular system.

CHICKEN TAGLIATELLE WITH ROASTED RED PEPPER SAUCE

The roasted red pepper sauce is a super-easy one to make and is absolutely delicious. It works amazingly well as a vegetarian dish, as well as with other meat and fish options – try swapping the chicken for mushrooms or prawns. It's also a great way to sneak vegetables into fussy eaters. Since the sauce is so versatile, it's worthwhile making an extra batch or two, cooling and freezing in individual portions in ziplock bags.

2 SERVES
15 PREP
25 COOK
597 CALORIES

2 LARGE RED PEPPERS, CORED, DESEEDED AND CHOPPED

1 LARGE RED ONION, ROUGHLY CHOPPED

2 GARLIC CLOVES, FINELY CHOPPED

OLIVE OIL

2 SKINLESS CHICKEN BREASTS

PINCH OF SMOKED PAPRIKA

150G DRIED TAGLIATELLE, PREFERABLY WHOLEWHEAT

SALT AND PEPPER

Preheat the oven to 180°C/160° fan/Gas Mark 4. Place the peppers, red onion and garlic in a roasting tin, drizzle with olive oil and season with salt and pepper, then toss together well. Roast for 20–25 minutes until all the vegetables are soft.

Once the vegetables are in the oven, place the chicken on a baking tray, sprinkle with the paprika and bake along with the roasting vegetables for 30–35 minutes until cooked through.

About halfway through the chicken baking time, place the tagliatelle in a large saucepan, cover with boiling water and simmer for about 10 minutes, or according to the packet instructions, until al dente (cooked but slightly firm). Drain, reserving a splash of the cooking water, and return to the hot pan.

Transfer the roasted vegetables to a food processor or blender and blitz into a smooth red sauce, adding a splash of water to loosen. Stir the sauce into the cooked tagliatelle and mix together well.

Slice or shred each cooked chicken breast into bite-sized pieces and add to the pasta, then divide everything between 2 bowls.

NUTRITION NUGGET
Peppers have a vitamin C content two to three times greater than citrus fruit!

MEDITERRANEAN ROASTED VEGETABLE AND FETA BOWL

This is somewhere between a nice side dish and a light lunch. If you wanted to make it a little more substantial, then add some cooked brown rice or quinoa, or even dollop it over a baked sweet potato.

1 SERVES · **15 PREP** · **30 COOK** · **503 CALORIES**

1 LARGE RED ONION, HALVED AND THICKLY SLICED LENGTHWAYS

1 LARGE COURGETTE, CHOPPED

1 RED PEPPER, CORED, DESEEDED AND CUT INTO LARGE CHUNKS

4 CHESTNUT MUSHROOMS, QUARTERED

¼ AUBERGINE, DICED

1 TABLESPOON OLIVE OIL

½ TEASPOON GARLIC SALT

½ TEASPOON SMOKED PAPRIKA

1 TEASPOON MIXED DRIED HERBS

85G FETA CHEESE

Preheat the oven to 220°C/200°C fan/Gas Mark 7.

Spread the prepared vegetables out in a roasting tin. Drizzle over the olive oil, sprinkle over the garlic salt, smoked paprika and dried herbs and toss together well.

Roast for 25–30 minutes, turning occasionally.

Transfer the roasted vegetables to a serving bowl and crumble over the feta.

NUTRITION NUGGET
Brightly coloured vegetables often contain colour pigments called carotenoids that can have many health benefits for the skin, cardiovascular system and eyes. These are fat-soluble substances, so combining them with a source of fat such as the feta cheese can increase their absorption, helping us to enjoy more of their beneficial properties.

SALMON AND AVOCADO RICE BOWL

Rice bowls such as Hawaiian poke bowls have become ultra on-trend in recent years. They are a great way to throw together healthy ingredients. For speed here, you could buy pre-cooked rice and pre-cooked salmon for a satisfying lunch on the hop.

1 SERVES · **10 PREP** · **30 COOK** · **921 CALORIES**

75G BROWN RICE

1 SKINLESS SALMON FILLET

OLIVE OIL

HANDFUL OF BABY SPINACH

½ AVOCADO, PEELED AND DICED

1 TABLESPOON COOKED FROZEN OR DRAINED CANNED EDAMAME (SOYA) BEANS

1 TEASPOON SESAME SEEDS

FOR THE DRESSING

1 TABLESPOON SOY SAUCE

2 TEASPOONS SESAME OIL

1 TEASPOON CLEAR HONEY

If you are cooking the salmon, preheat the oven to 190°C/170°C fan/Gas Mark 5.

While the oven is heating up, place the rice in a saucepan, cover with boiling water and simmer for about 30–40 minutes until tender and fluffy.

Place the salmon on an oiled baking tray and bake for about 15 minutes until the flesh of the fish flakes easily when prodded with a fork.

Meanwhile, heat a little olive oil in a pan, add the baby spinach and sauté until wilted.

When the rice is ready, drain and tip into a serving bowl. Flake the cooked salmon over it in one area, place the diced avocado in another, the cooked spinach in another and the edamame beans in another so that each ingredient occupies its own little space on top of the rice. Sprinkle over the sesame seeds.

Mix the ingredients for the dressing together in a small bowl, then pour the dressing over all the ingredients in the bowl.

NUTRITION NUGGET
Avocados are a great source of vitamin E, which has antioxidant properties as well as benefits for the cardiovascular system.

SWEET TREATS

CHAPTER

7

I have to be honest here, I really don't have a sweet tooth, and boy I'm glad I don't, as I think I would be in trouble otherwise. In general, I can't advocate eating sweet things and I often laugh at the notion that 'natural' sugar isn't bad for you. Sugar is sugar and we MUST be careful with it, however it's packaged. That being said, one of the key aims of this book is to help you transition into healthier eating habits. So if you are going to have something sweet, then I would much rather we give these foods some kind of facelift and make them as healthy as they can be.

These recipes will help you to scratch that sweet itch but without causing too many problems. This doesn't, though, give you a free pass to eat a whole batch in a day. The main purpose here is to try and minimize the negatives associated with your regular shop-bought sweet treats.

THE
EAT
SHOP
SAV£
WAY

Mars Bar =
260 calories
35g sugar

Crunchy Chocolate
Trail Bark (page 170) =
172 calories per portion
8.2g sugar

Additional benefits include:
A great source of
» Magnesium
» Iron
» Zinc
» Copper
» Manganese
» Omega-3 fatty acids

NUTRITION NUGGET

My Crunchy Chocolate Trail Bark is not only delicious but just look at the difference in sugar content compared to a Mars Bar! We all know that we should be cutting down on our sugar intake, and this superfood-packed treat is just the ticket, satisfying even the sweetest tooth. The protein and fibre content of the sunflower seeds and flaxseeds will stave off hunger (perfect for that mid-afternoon slump), and will have less of an effect on blood sugar levels compared to sugar-laden sweet treats. And as we know, balanced blood sugar is hugely important when it comes to long-term health.

Sunflower seeds are high in vitamin E, the body's primary fat-soluble antioxidant. Vitamin E travels throughout the body neutralizing free radicals that would otherwise damage fat-containing structures and molecules, such as cell membranes and cholesterol. By protecting these components, vitamin E has significant anti-inflammatory effects. Sunflower seeds are also an excellent source of copper, vitamin B1, selenium and magnesium. Flaxseeds are an important source of omega-3 fatty acids for anyone with a plant-based diet. They are also a good source of vitamin B1, copper and manganese.

SEEDY BANANA PEANUT BUTTER OAT COOKIES

I used to make banana oat bars years ago and this recipe is an evolution of those. Super easy and super tasty, the winning combination of banana and peanut butter is timeless. Just make sure you get the type of peanut butter that doesn't have sugar and other unwanted additives in it.

8-10 MAKES
15 PREP
20 COOK
178 CALORIES

2 VERY RIPE BANANAS (LOOK FOR BROWN SPOTS ON THE SKIN)

4 TABLESPOONS CRUNCHY PEANUT BUTTER

3 TEASPOONS CLEAR HONEY

2 TEASPOONS BUTTER

150G PORRIDGE OATS

3 TEASPOONS MIXED SEEDS

Preheat the oven to 180°C/160°C fan/Gas Mark 4 and line 1 large or 2 smaller baking sheets with greaseproof paper.

Peel the bananas and break up into a bowl. Add the peanut butter, honey and butter and mash together well with a fork.

Add the oats and seeds and stir together until you have a sticky dough mixture.

Break the dough off into 8–10 equal-sized balls. Place the balls spaced out on the lined sheet(s) and then flatten and shape them into cookies.

Bake for 15–20 minutes until golden brown. Once cooled, store in an airtight container.

NUTRITION NUGGET
While these are quite carb-heavy and contain honey, the fibre in the oats and the protein in the peanut butter will at least slow down the release of the sugars.

CRUNCHY CHOCOLATE TRAIL BARK

I know this sounds a bit like a bushtucker trial, but the bark in this case is a thin shard of chocolate that you can embed with all sorts of nutritious ingredients. This combination has a trail mix vibe to it. And the good news...chocolate can be incredibly good for you. Winner!

 4 SERVINGS

 15 PREP 1 HOUR CHILL

 60 CHILL **172 CALORIES**

100G 70% COCOA DARK CHOCOLATE

1 TABLESPOON PUMPKIN SEEDS

1 TABLESPOON GOJI BERRIES

1 TEASPOON SUNFLOWER SEEDS

1 TEASPOON FLAXSEEDS

Break the chocolate into a heatproof bowl. Set the bowl over a saucepan half-filled with just-boiled water but OFF the heat. Stir continuously until melted.

Line a baking tray with greaseproof paper. Pour the melted chocolate on to the lined tray and spread it out to form a thin even layer.

Sprinkle all the seeds and berries randomly over the melted chocolate. Then place the tray in the fridge for an hour until set.

Break the chocolate off into shards and store in an airtight container in the fridge.

NUTRITION NUGGET

There is cheering news in the world folks. Chocolate is GOOD for you. But let me qualify that statement slightly. Cocoa is rich in flavonoids, which help lower blood pressure, protect the cardiovascular system from damage and improve circulation to the brain. It's also a rich source of magnesium. But you must opt for dark chocolate with a high percentage of cocoa to get these benefits.

PEARS POACHED IN SPICED RED WINE

There is something just a little bit posh about poached pears, and anything with red wine involved is always a winner. This lovely flavoursome dessert is a great one to pull out at a dinner party and gets some fruit into you too!

4 SERVES | 10 PREP | 35 COOK | 219 CALORIES

75CL BOTTLE RED WINE (CHEAP STUFF – NO CHÂTEAU MARGAUX HERE!)

4 TABLESPOONS CLEAR HONEY

2 LARGE CINNAMON STICKS

3 STAR ANISE

1 TEASPOON VANILLA EXTRACT

4 PEARS, PEELED

VANILLA YOGURT, TO SERVE

Place the wine, honey, spices and vanilla extract in a deep-sided saucepan and gently heat until you see steam rising from it.

Gently lower in the pears, cover the pan and simmer for 25–30 minutes.

Serve with vanilla yogurt.

NUTRITION NUGGET
Pears contain a fibre called pectin. This forms a gel-like substance in the gut that helps to improve digestive transit as well as support gut flora and even lower cholesterol.

RAW BROWNIES

These are another of those items that have started to pop up everywhere, but again they are super expensive in the shops in comparison to how much they cost to make. You could use any combination of nuts, but I've found this one to be the tastiest.

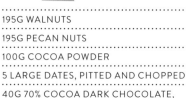

195G WALNUTS

195G PECAN NUTS

100G COCOA POWDER

5 LARGE DATES, PITTED AND CHOPPED

40G 70% COCOA DARK CHOCOLATE, FINELY CHOPPED

3 TABLESPOONS MAPLE SYRUP

1 TABLESPOON COCONUT OIL, MELTED

GRATED ZEST OF 1 ORANGE (OPTIONAL)

Place the nuts, cocoa and dates in a food processor and blitz to a fine grainy texture.

Add the chocolate, maple syrup and coconut oil and mix well until the mixture sticks together and becomes like a dough.

Line a baking tray with greaseproof paper, tip in the mixture and press down firmly into an evenly compacted layer.

Place in the fridge for at least 3–4 hours, preferably overnight, before cutting into squares. Store in an airtight container in the fridge.

NUTRITION NUGGET
Using ingredients raw as in these brownies helps to keep many of their important nutrients intact, especially the oils and fat-soluble nutrients such as vitamin E.

BAKED FIGS WITH GINGER YOGURT AND SEEDS

This is a gorgeously light, summery dessert, and it couldn't be simpler to prepare. I adore figs – I'm actually sitting here staring straight at my fig tree as I write.

1 SERVES

10 PREP

20 COOK

333 CALORIES

2 RIPE FIGS

½ TEASPOON CLEAR HONEY

3 TABLESPOONS VANILLA YOGURT

2.5CM PIECE OF FRESH ROOT GINGER, PEELED AND GRATED

1 TABLESPOON MIXED SEEDS

Preheat the oven to 180°C/160°C fan/Gas Mark 4 and line a small baking tray with greaseproof paper.

Slice the figs lengthways in half and place cut side up in the lined baking tray. Drizzle the honey over them. Bake for 20 minutes.

Meanwhile, mix the vanilla yogurt and grated ginger together.

Place the yogurt in a serving bowl, top with the figs and any caramel from the tin, then sprinkle over the seeds.

NUTRITION NUGGET
Figs are a great source of dietary fibre and also contain small amounts of substances called anthraquinone glycosides that can regulate digestive transit.

HONEY ROASTED CASHEWS

These are a great portable sweet snack that can be a handy lunch-box filler. Because the nuts are composed almost entirely of protein and healthy fats, the sweetness won't disrupt blood sugar, and a small handful is enough for a serving.

8 PORTIONS
10 PREP
30 COOK
190 CALORIES

250G RAW CASHEW NUTS

2 TEASPOONS CLEAR HONEY

1 TEASPOON GROUND CINNAMON

Preheat the oven to 180°C/160°C fan/Gas Mark 4. Line a baking sheet with greaseproof paper.

Place the cashew nuts in a bowl. Drizzle over the honey and mix together well so that the nuts are covered. Sprinkle over the cinnamon and mix well again to ensure that the nuts are fully coated.

Spread the coated nuts out evenly on the lined baking sheet to form a single layer. Roast for 25–30 minutes until golden brown, turning occasionally.

Leave to cool before eating – they will be sticky when warm but turn crunchier once cooled. Store in an airtight container.

NUTRITION NUGGET
Cashew nuts are a great non-dairy source of calcium.

CHOCOLATE CHICKPEA BARS

OK, I know this recipe sounds...unconventional, but the chickpeas work as a great flour alternative and add a big protein hit to these bars.

10 MAKES

15 PREP

30 COOK

180 CALORIES

400G CAN CHICKPEAS, DRAINED

125G ALMOND BUTTER

80ML MAPLE SYRUP

2 TEASPOONS COCOA POWDER

¼ TEASPOON BICARBONATE OF SODA

¼ TEASPOON BAKING POWDER

60G DARK CHOCOLATE CHIPS

Preheat the oven to 180°C/160°C fan/Gas Mark 4. Line a baking tray with greaseproof paper.

Place all the ingredients except the chocolate chips in a food processor and blitz until smooth. Add the chocolate chips and mix together well.

Tip the mixture into the lined tray, spread out into an even layer and bake for 25–30 minutes.

Leave to cool completely before cutting into bars. Store in an airtight container.

NUTRITION NUGGET
Chickpeas are an excellent source of B vitamins, zinc and fibre.

BAKED APPLE AND BANANA WITH OATY CRUMBLE TOP AND BOTTOM

A bit like a double-layered crumble, this dessert is a great way to get extra fresh fruit into your diet and up your fibre intake. The banana goes all gooey in this one too. Gorgeous stuff!

1 SERVES | 10 PREP | 25 COOK | 377 CALORIES

1 APPLE, CORED AND CUT INTO WEDGES

1 RIPE BANANA

1 TEASPOON CLEAR HONEY

4 TABLESPOONS PORRIDGE OATS

1 TEASPOON GROUND CINNAMON

Preheat the oven to 180°C/160°C fan/Gas Mark 4.

Place the apple wedges on a baking tray. Peel and break the banana into chunks and add to the tray, then drizzle the fruit with the honey. Bake for 20–25 minutes until the fruit is soft and gooey.

Mix the oats and cinnamon together in a bowl, ensuring they are well combined.

Place 2 tablespoons of the cinnamon oat mixture into the bottom a serving bowl. Top with the baked fruit, then sprinkle over the remaining cinnamon oat mixture before serving.

NUTRITION NUGGET
Oats are a great source of biotin, a nutrient that promotes healthy, bright skin.

GINGER DATE BALLS

Energy balls are so on-trend right now, but the cost of the pre-prepared ones you find in the shops is absolutely laughable when they are so cheap and easy to make yourself.

24 MAKES | 15 PREP | 100 CALORIES

250G PITTED DATES, CHOPPED

250G WALNUTS

1 HEAPED TEASPOON GROUND CINNAMON

½ TEASPOON GROUND GINGER

DESICCATED COCONUT, FOR COATING (OPTIONAL)

Place all the ingredients in a food processor and blitz into a stiff paste.

Break off 5cm pieces of the paste and roll into balls.

These are great as they are or you could roll them in desiccated coconut to jazz them up a bit.

Store in an airtight container in the fridge.

NUTRITION NUGGET
Walnuts are one of the richest food sources of zinc.

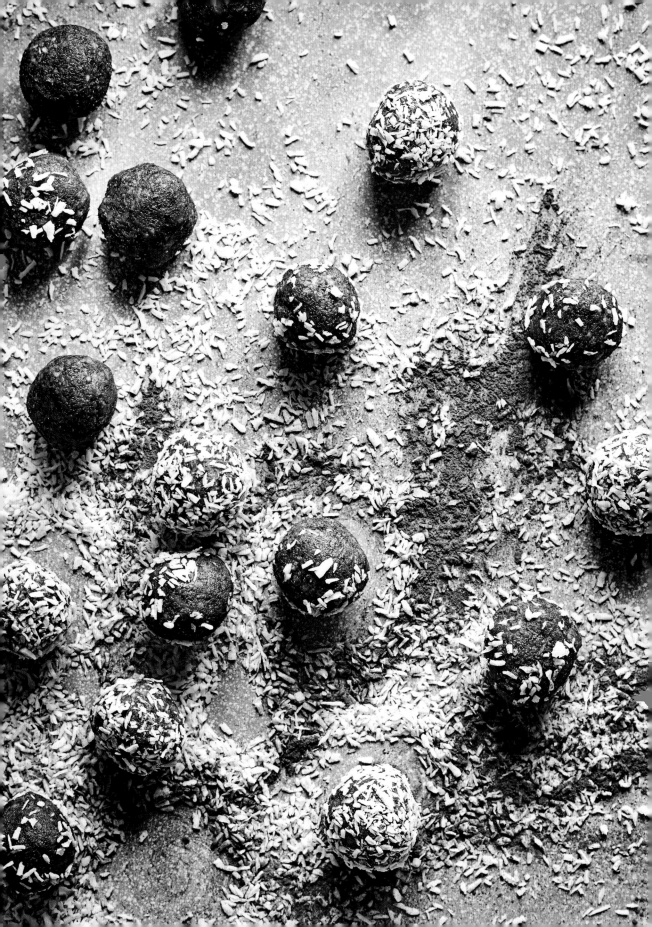

FRIDGE BARS

These are another of those sweet treats that are insanely easy to make and are perfectly portable, making them a great option to take to work or school. They are filling and contain a lot of important nutrients to boot.

10 SERVES

15 PREP

4 HOURS CHILL

240 CALORIES

100G DATES, PITTED AND CHOPPED

100G SESAME SEEDS

100G PUMPKIN SEEDS

50G DESICCATED COCONUT

2 TABLESPOONS CLEAR HONEY

2 TABLESPOONS TAHINI

1 TABLESPOON COCONUT OIL

Place all the ingredients in a food processor and blitz into a rough dough-like texture.

Line a small square baking tin with greaseproof paper. Tip the mixture into the tin and press down firmly into an evenly compacted layer.

Refrigerate for 3–4 hours before cutting into bars. Store in an airtight container in the fridge.

NUTRITION NUGGET
Seeds such as pumpkin seeds are a great source of several important nutrients. They are rich in the minerals zinc and selenium, zinc being vital for effective immunity and healthy skin, and selenium for cellular repair. These types of seed are also valuable sources of antioxidant vitamin E.

MEAL PLANNERS

Here are some sample meal planners, using recipes from the book, to help you plan a week of evening meals. To make it even easier, I've included a list of all the ingredients you'll need. Each list of foods is enough for four people for that week, so feel free to adapt it to your needs. Each week has at least two plant-based meals and at least two meals under 500 calories, so you'll easily reap the benefits of the whole book.

WEEK 1

MONDAY
FIG AND FETA SALAD
PAGE 38
UNDER 500 CALORIES

A little beauty that has summer written all over it, this is a glorious collision of sweet and salty that's perfect as a main dish or served as an accompaniment to a barbecue.

TUESDAY
BEETROOT AND HORSERADISH
PAGE 16
UNDER 500 CALORIES

If you haven't tried this flavour combination, do give it a go – this could become one of your new favourite taste sensations. And if that's the case, it's easy to store any extra portions in the freezer.

WEDNESDAY
WARM STEAK SALAD
PAGE 60

This gorgeous dish is perfect as a lunch, or a summertime evening meal. It's heaven for me and typical of the sort of fare I reach for regularly. Although the recipe is for one, it's easy to multiply up.

THURSDAY
SUN-DRIED TOMATO, COURGETTE AND RED PEPPER RISOTTO
PAGE 126

I've pimped up the classic risotto here, nutritionally speaking, by swapping the usual short-grain white rice for brown.

FRIDAY
PAD THAI UPGRADED
PAGE 156

I do love a good pad Thai, but it can often be swimming in refined sugar, and have little vegetable content beyond a tickle with a couple of bean sprouts. I have had some far more adventurous versions in Thailand, and with a bit of pimping up it can be a healthy light meal. You can swap the prawns for tofu and it works just as well.

WEEK 1 SHOPPING LIST

FRESH
400G OF YOUR PREFERRED CUT OF STEAK

560G UNCOOKED PEELED KING PRAWNS

4 EGGS

320G FETA CHEESE

4 TABLESPOONS GREEK YOGURT

13 HANDFULS OF BABY SPINACH

4 COURGETTES

7 RED ONIONS

8 HANDFULS OF MIXED SALAD LEAVES

4 HANDFULS OF ROCKET

4 SMALL HANDFULS OF CHERRY TOMATOES

4 CARROTS

18 GARLIC CLOVES

4 X 250G VACUUM PACKS COOKED BEETROOT (NOT THE PICKLED KIND)

4 RED PEPPERS

8 FRESH FIGS

3 TEASPOONS LEMON JUICE

2 LIMES

4 GREEN CHILLIES

12–16 SPRING ONIONS

CUPBOARD
OLIVE OIL

2 TEASPOONS DRIED OREGANO OR MIXED DRIED HERBS

SALT AND PEPPER

2.8L VEGETABLE STOCK

5 TABLESPOONS HORSERADISH SAUCE

4 TEASPOONS MAYONNAISE

4 TEASPOONS BALSAMIC VINEGAR

2 TEASPOONS ENGLISH MUSTARD

120G SUN-DRIED TOMATOES IN OIL

500G SHORT-GRAIN BROWN RICE

2 X 400G CANS CHOPPED TOMATOES

75G DRIED FLAT RICE NOODLES

5 TEASPOONS CLEAR HONEY

8 TEASPOONS FISH SAUCE OR SOY SAUCE

4 TABLESPOONS PEANUTS

WEEK 2 SHOPPING LIST

FRESH

4 EGGS

4 LARGE SKINLESS CHICKEN BREASTS

160G FETA CHEESE

120G FULL-FAT SOFT CHEESE

4 RIVER COBBLER (BASA) FILLETS

2 SMALL BEETROOTS

4 LARGE CARROTS

1 LARGE CAULIFLOWER

4 LARGE HANDFULS OF SHREDDED SPRING GREENS

12 NEW POTATOES

4 SMALL HANDFULS OF GREEN BEANS

4 LITTLE GEM LETTUCES OR 2 COS LETTUCES

8 LARGE TOMATOES

11 GARLIC CLOVES

1 LARGE RED ONION

5CM PIECE OF FRESH ROOT GINGER

1KG BUTTERNUT SQUASH

4 HANDFULS OF ROCKET

4 ROSEMARY SPRIGS (OPTIONAL)

480G MUSHROOMS

2 LIMES

CUPBOARD

OLIVE OIL

8 TEASPOONS BALSAMIC VINEGAR

2 TEASPOONS SMOKED PAPRIKA

2 TEASPOONS GARLIC SALT

1 TEASPOON GROUND CUMIN

240G DRAINED CANNED TUNA

16 ANCHOVY FILLETS

24–28 PITTED BLACK OLIVES

4 TABLESPOONS RED WINE VINEGAR

2 TEASPOONS DIJON MUSTARD

800ML VEGETABLE STOCK

800G COOKED FROZEN OR DRAINED CANNED BROAD BEANS

SALT AND PEPPER

TO SERVE

THURSDAY: WILTED GREENS AND SWEET POTATO MASH

WEEK 2

MONDAY
CAULIFLOWER 'STEAK' WITH BALSAMIC ROOT ROAST
PAGE 134

UNDER 500 CALORIES

Who would have thought it... cauliflower steak has become 'a thing'!

TUESDAY
CLASSIC NIÇOISE SALAD
PAGE 40

The Niçoise is one of those timeless recipes that just never becomes tired or goes out of fashion. You will find this ultimate classic salad on most summer menus, but it's one that's easy to re-create at home.

WEDNESDAY
GINGERED SQUASH SOUP
PAGE 16

`UNDER 500 CALORIES`

A classic combination: the sweetness of the squash and the zing of the ginger make such an amazing contrast in this soup. It's a taste explosion! This is an ideal candidate for batch cooking and freezing.

THURSDAY
CHICKEN WITH PEPPERED MUSHROOM SAUCE
PAGE 62

An elegant yet comforting dish, this is a total doddle to make, taking very little time at all to knock together.

FRIDAY
RIVER COBBLER WITH BROAD BEAN MASH AND LIME ROCKET SALAD
PAGE 90

River cobbler, sometimes called basa, is a cheap alternative to cod. It is equally as tasty and has the same type of texture, and can be used in just the same way.

WEEK 3

MONDAY
ROASTED RED ONION, BEETROOT AND GOATS CHEESE SALAD
PAGE 34

UNDER 500 CALORIES

This is a flavour combination that I absolutely adore. You can prep the onions ahead of time so that you can just throw this salad together when you fancy it. Having said that, I personally prefer it when the onions are warm, as they contrast with the goats' cheese beautifully.

TUESDAY
VIBRANT VICHYSSOISE
PAGE 18

UNDER 500 CALORIES

Vichyssoise is one of those all-time classics that is adored by everyone, which very definitely includes me. My version takes the already goodness-packed recipe and gives it even more nutritional value. As with most soups, this freezes well.

WEDNESDAY
IMAM BAYILDI
PAGE 136

UNDER 500 CALORIES

The name of this classic Turkish recipe translates as 'the imam fainted', due to the overwhelming deliciousness of the dish, so the legend goes!

THURSDAY
MAPLE MUSTARD SALMON WITH PAPRIKA SWEET POTATO WEDGES AND GREEN SALAD
PAGE 106

Such a wonderful marriage of flavours, this dish is super filling and very straightforward to make.

FRIDAY
CHINESE ROAST CHICKEN
PAGE 70

Blast your Sunday roasts into orbit with this delicious twist on roast chicken! Beautifully aromatic and flavoursome, when people smell this dish cooking, they will come running. It does, however, need prepping in advance to achieve that maximum flavour hit.

WEEK 3 SHOPPING LIST

FRESH
170G SOFT GOATS' CHEESE
4 SALMON FILLETS
1 MEDIUM CHICKEN, ABOUT 1.5KG
4 RED ONIONS
1 LARGE ONION
9 GARLIC CLOVES
300G LEEKS
110G POTATO
3 LARGE HANDFULS OF CURLY KALE
6 TABLESPOONS GARDEN PEAS (FRESH OR FROZEN)
4 AUBERGINES
2 LARGE SWEET POTATOES
4 HANDFULS OF BABY SPINACH
6 SPRING ONIONS
4 HANDFULS OF SUGAR SNAP PEAS
2 LIMES
4 LARGE HANDFULS OF MIXED SALAD LEAVES (THE DARKER THE BETTER)
2 COOKED BEETROOT
8–10 CHERRY TOMATOES
1 TEASPOON DRIED MIXED HERBS

CUPBOARD
OLIVE OIL
9 TEASPOONS CLEAR HONEY
4 TEASPOONS BALSAMIC VINEGAR
600ML VEGETABLE STOCK
800G CHOPPED TOMATOES
4 TEASPOONS GROUND CINNAMON
4 TABLESPOONS MAPLE SYRUP
4 TEASPOONS WHOLEGRAIN MUSTARD
6 TEASPOONS SESAME OIL
2 TEASPOONS TOASTED SESAME OIL
2 TEASPOON SMOKED PAPRIKA
1 TEASPOON GARLIC SALT
3 TABLESPOONS LIGHT SOY SAUCE
1 TEASPOON CHINESE FIVE-SPICE POWDER
SALT AND PEPPER

TO SERVE
WEDNESDAY: SALAD, TO SERVE
FRIDAY: GREEN SALAD

WEEK 4
SHOPPING LIST

FRESH

4 SKINLESS CHICKEN BREASTS

4 TABLESPOONS GRATED PARMESAN CHEESE

20–24 ANCHOVY FILLETS

120G FETA CHEESE

2 SKINLESS SALMON FILLETS

2 SKINLESS COD FILLETS

8 LARGE HANDFULS OF CURLY KALE

16–20 CHERRY TOMATOES

4 CELERY STICKS

5 RED ONIONS

1 LARGE ONION

9 GARLIC CLOVES

150G WHITE MUSHROOMS

150G CHESTNUT MUSHROOMS

150G SHIITAKE MUSHROOMS

4 PARSNIPS

4 CARROTS

4 BEETROOT

2 LARGE COURGETTES

10–12 HANDFULS OF BABY SPINACH

2 LEMONS

2 LARGE LEMON GRASS STALKS

1 GREEN CHILLI

CUPBOARD

OLIVE OIL

300G DRIED WHOLEWHEAT PENNE

150G SUN-DRIED TOMATO PASTE

1 TABLESPOON PLAIN FLOUR

1L VEGETABLE STOCK

2 TEASPOONS DRIED MIXED HERBS

½ TEASPOON GROUND CUMIN

½ TEASPOON GROUND CINNAMON

2 X 400G CAN CANNELLINI BEANS

2 TABLESPOONS TAHINI

250G DRIED RED LENTILS

400ML CAN COCONUT MILK

SALT AND PEPPER

WEEK 4

MONDAY
KALE, PARMESAN, CHICKEN AND ANCHOVY SALAD
PAGE 42

`UNDER 500 CALORIES`

This little bad boy is an absolute flavour bomb. With this much protein, fibre and healthy fats, it's super satisfying too, so you won't be reaching for the snack drawer later in the day.

TUESDAY
VEGGIE PACKED PENNE WITH FETA
PAGE 152

This is one of my absolute favourite comfort foods. If it's freezing cold outside or if I'm just feeling a bit down in the dumps, a bowl of this is the best tonic. There is just something so soothing about it, and it's packed with the good stuff too! Sun-dried tomato paste is now easy to find in jars in most supermarkets.

WEDNESDAY
THREE MUSHROOM SOUP
PAGE 20

UNDER 500 CALORIES

When I first went into nutrition, one of my early obsessions was mushrooms, which might sound dodgy on the face of it, but there are certain varieties of mushroom that can have some incredibly positive influences on immunity. They are also a great source of vitamin D.

THURSDAY
ROASTED ROOTS WITH WHITE BEAN PUREE
PAGE 128

UNDER 500 CALORIES

This is such a beautiful and filling dish. As well as having a wonderfully satisfying texture contrast, it has an amazing nutritional profile.

FRIDAY
FANCY FISH CURRY
PAGE 94

This is an interesting fusion-type curry. Imagine the texture of the lentil-based Indian dishes dhansak or dhal crossed with the flavour profile of a Thai curry. That's what we have here, and it tastes out of this world.

WEEK 5

MONDAY
GREEN PASTA
PAGE 148

This pasta looks, well, a bit weird at first, but man alive, the flavour! In reality you can use almost anything in the sauce to enhance the taste, but these ingredients keep to the classic Italian flavour profile. Having said that, anything goes in cooking these days, so feel free to get adventurous.

TUESDAY
DREAMY CREAMY CAULIFLOWER SOUP
PAGE 22

UNDER 500 CALORIES

Up until a couple of years ago, I used to think that cauliflower was the devil's food. I couldn't stand it – apart from in a soup. Trust me, its flavour is transformed and the texture it gives is absolutely gorgeous.

WEDNESDAY
SMOKED MACKEREL SALAD
PAGE 52

This is a flavour fest and no mistake, containing an enormous array of nutrients. The dressing is quite something too – vivid green and bursting with fiery, zingy flavour.

THURSDAY
SALMON AND AVOCADO RICE BOWL
PAGE 162

Rice bowls such as Hawaiian poke bowls have become ultra on-trend in recent years. They are a great way to throw together healthy ingredients. For speed here, you could buy pre-cooked rice and pre-cooked salmon for a satisfying lunch on the hop.

FRIDAY
BEEF, BROCCOLI AND GINGER STIR-FRY
PAGE 66

UNDER 500 CALORIES

Stir-fries really are one of the staples of healthier cooking. They give you the opportunity to throw together all manner of amazing fresh ingredients and cook them quickly and in a way that retains many of the beneficial nutrients they contain.

WEEK 5 SHOPPING LIST

FRESH
4 SMOKED MACKEREL FILLETS
200ML SINGLE CREAM
4 SKINNED SALMON FILLETS
500G PRE-CUT BEEF STRIPS
3 ONIONS
12 GARLIC CLOVES
8–10 HANDFULS OF FROZEN PEAS
60G BASIL
60G FLAT LEAF PARSLEY
6 LARGE COURGETTES
800G CAULIFLOWER FLORETS
4 LARGE HANDFULS OF WATERCRESS
6 VERY RIPE AVOCADOS
4 LEMONS
4 HANDFULS OF BABY SPINACH
4 TABLESPOONS COOKED FROZEN OR DRAINED CANNED EDAMAME (SOYA) BEANS
5CM PIECE OF FRESH ROOT GINGER
1 LARGE HEAD OF BROCCOLI

CUPBOARD
800ML VEGETABLE STOCK
400ML CAN COCONUT MILK
8 HEAPED TEASPOONS HOT HORSERADISH SAUCE
300G DRIED WHOLEWHEAT FUSILLI
300G BROWN RICE
4 TABLESPOONS SESAME SEEDS
4 TABLESPOONS SOY SAUCE
8 TEASPOONS SESAME OIL
4 TEASPOONS CLEAR HONEY
1 TABLESPOON SESAME OIL
3 TABLESPOONS CHINESE OYSTER SAUCE
OLIVE OIL
SALT AND PEPPER

TO SERVE
FRIDAY: BROWN RICE, TO SERVE

WEEK 6 SHOPPING LIST

FRESH

280G GOATS' CHEESE LOG

4 SKINLESS SALMON FILLETS

8 HIGH-QUALITY PORK SAUSAGES

7 LARGE RED ONIONS

11 GARLIC CLOVES

2 LARGE COURGETTES

2 LARGE RED PEPPERS

4–6 CHESTNUT MUSHROOMS

6 LARGE HANDFULS
OF MIXED SALAD

LEAVES

2 SMALL BUTTERNUT SQUASH

3 HANDFULS OF BABY SPINACH

BASIL OR PARSLEY (OPTIONAL)

SMALL BUNCH OF CORIANDER
(OPTIONAL)

15–20G SAGE

1 LEMON

CUPBOARD

OLIVE OIL

4 TEASPOONS SMOKED PAPRIKA

1 TEASPOON GARLIC SALT

2 TEASPOONS DRIED MIXED HERBS

200G DRIED RED LENTILS

1.2L VEGETABLE STOCK

2 X 400G CANS BUTTER BEANS

400G CAN TOMATOES

400G CAN CANNELLINI BEANS

2 TABLESPOONS MAYONNAISE

1 TEASPOON MEDIUM CHILLI POWDER

4 WHOLEWHEAT OR MULTIGRAIN BUNS

SALT AND PEPPER

WEEK 6

MONDAY
GOAT'S CHEESE AND ROASTED VEGETABLE SALAD
PAGE 44

`UNDER 500 CALORIES`

A firm favourite in my house, this gorgeous salad is at its best served warm, but the roasted veggies will keep perfectly well in the fridge for adding cold to a salad the next day, or as a great sandwich filler with some hummus.

TUESDAY
RED LENTIL, WHITE BEAN AND BUTTERNUT SQUASH STEW
PAGE 116

Perfect as a warming winter dish, this recipe gives you a bowl full of feel-good factor. It's simple one-pot cooking at its absolute best, and an ideal candidate for doubling up the quantities and freezing for an effortless meal at a later date.

WEDNESDAY
TOMATO AND WHITE BEAN SOUP
PAGE 24

`UNDER 500 CALORIES`

This soup is such a doddle to make (and so speedy, it's hardly worth making extra for freezing), besides being as cheap as chips, using everyday ingredients. It's also packed with antioxidants and minerals.

THURSDAY
SAUSAGE, SAGE AND SQUASH ONE-TRAY ROAST
PAGE 64

`UNDER 500 CALORIES`

One-tray roasts and bakes are a beautiful and effortless way to cook in the colder months. The flavours fully develop and fuse together well with areas of inviting caramelization, resulting in something warming and hearty. Lovely!

FRIDAY
SALMON BURGERS WITH CHILLI AIOLI
PAGE 96

These gorgeous burgers are a great midweek treat. Weirdly, they don't taste very fishy at all, and end up very meaty, so it's a perfect dish for those who are timid about eating fish.

WEEK 7

MONDAY
THAI-STYLE VEGGIE 'NOODLE' SALAD
PAGE 50

`UNDER 500 CALORIES`

It's official...vegetable noodles have become 'a thing'. I have had one of those spiralizer contraptions since the 1990s – back then we were mavericks! But now, thanks to the huge popularity of veggie noodles, you no longer have to grapple with such a gadget, as they are available pre-prepared in your supermarket. Winner!

TUESDAY
SWEET POTATO AND APPLE SOUP
PAGE 24

`UNDER 500 CALORIES`

This combo may sound weird, but my word does it work well! It makes a seriously satisfying soup that is truly unforgettable.

WEDNESDAY
TURKEY STUFFED PEPPERS
PAGE 68

`UNDER 500 CALORIES`

This is a wonderfully simple supper idea, and also ideal for an easy make-ahead lunch.

THURSDAY
NUTTY NOODLES
PAGE 122

This recipe could have quite easily gone into the Bowl Food section of the book, but it's such a shining example of how delicious vegan/plant-based food can be that I just had to put it in here. A sure-fire candidate for a future food addiction!

FRIDAY
CHILLI PRAWNS WITH RED ONION AND COURGETTES
PAGE 100

UNDER 500 CALORIES

This is a dead easy dish that makes a speedy lunch or dinner when you want something fresh and tasty but don't want to wait an hour and a half for the pleasure.

WEEK 7 SHOPPING LIST

FRESH

500G TURKEY MINCE

2 TABLESPOONS FULL-FAT SOFT CHEESE

350G UNCOOKED PEELED KING PRAWNS

4 HANDFULS OF PRE-PREPARED CARROT NOODLES

4 HANDFULS OF PRE-PREPARED COURGETTE NOODLES

1 BUNCH OF CORIANDER

4 LIMES

15 GARLIC CLOVES

5 RED CHILLIES

2 ½ LARGE RED ONIONS

800G SWEET POTATOES

1 LARGE GREEN APPLE

2 LARGE RED PEPPERS

5–6 SHIITAKE MUSHROOMS

2 COURGETTES

CUPBOARD

OLIVE OIL

4 TABLESPOONS CASHEW NUTS

8 TEASPOONS SOY SAUCE

4 TEASPOONS SESAME OIL

750ML VEGETABLE STOCK

1 TEASPOON DRIED MIXED HERBS

50G DRIED FLAT RICE NOODLES

1 HEAPED TABLESPOON CRUNCHY PEANUT BUTTER

2 TEASPOONS SOY SAUCE

2 ½ TEASPOON CLEAR HONEY

6–8 DICED PIECES OF FIRM TOFU

½ TEASPOON SMOKED PAPRIKA

SALT AND PEPPER

TO SERVE

WEDNESDAY: SALAD AND BROWN RICE OR QUINOA

FRIDAY: NOODLES OR BROWN RICE

WEEK 8
SHOPPING LIST

FRESH

8 TABLESPOONS NATURAL YOGURT

260G STRONG BLUE CHEESE

4 SALMON FILLETS

4 SKINLESS CHICKEN BREASTS

4 LARGE RED ONIONS

17 GARLIC CLOVES

500G BABY SPINACH

4 LARGE PEACHES

4 GENEROUS HANDFULS
OF WATERCRESS

400G CARROTS

400G CAULIFLOWER FLORETS

2 GREEN CHILLIES

4CM PIECE OF FRESH ROOT GINGER

2 LIMES

3 LARGE SPRING ONIONS

SMALL HANDFUL OF CORIANDER
LEAVES (OPTIONAL)

CUPBOARD

OLIVE OIL

2 TABLESPOONS CURRY PASTE
(HOW HOT IS UP TO YOU)

2 X 400G CAN CHOPPED TOMATOES

2 X 400G CANS CHICKPEAS

1 TEASPOON GROUND CUMIN

1 TEASPOON FENNEL SEEDS

2 TEASPOONS SESAME OIL

3 TABLESPOONS PEANUT BUTTER

1 TEASPOON CHINESE
FIVE-SPICE POWDER

2 TEASPOONS CLEAR HONEY

2 TEASPOONS SOY SAUCE

SALT AND PEPPER

TO SERVE

MONDAY: BROWN RICE

THURSDAY: BROWN RICE
AND STIR-FRIED GREENS

FRIDAY: BROWN RICE
OR WILTED GREENS

WEEK 8

MONDAY
SPEEDY CHICKPEA AND SPINACH CURRY
PAGE 132

Speedy, simple yet flavoursome, this is a great dish for when you really can't be bothered to spend ages in the kitchen, but want something decent. Winner, winner chickpea dinner!

TUESDAY
PEACH, BLUE CHEESE AND WATERCRESS SALAD
PAGE 48

UNDER 500 CALORIES

Ok...I've gone into the weird zone again. Believe me, though, when I say that this is a salad to impress. Bring this out at a barbecue and, once your friends have finished scratching their heads in bewilderment, they will take one taste and get their minds blown. It's worth making just for the reaction! I say making, but this salad is simply an assembly job.

WEDNESDAY
ROASTED CARROT AND CAULIFLOWER SOUP
PAGE 22

`UNDER 500 CALORIES`

The pre-roasting of the vegetables here brings an extra flavour dimension, with the spices bringing a warm toastiness.

THURSDAY
CHILLI AND LIME SALMON PARCELS
PAGE 102

`UNDER 500 CALORIES`

As simple as it gets, this is the ideal way of cooking fish if you need a quick and healthy, throw-together meal after a long day. You can concoct every conceivable flavour combination you fancy, and it keeps the prepping of ingredients to a minimum, not to mention saving on the washing-up!

FRIDAY
CHICKEN WITH SPRING ONIONS IN SATAY SAUCE
PAGE 74

`UNDER 500 CALORIES`

An absolute belter of a dish, this has so much flavour and a divine richness. If you have fussy eaters in the house, it can be absolute gold dust.

INDEX

all the blues 26
anchovies
  classic Niçoise salad 40
  kale, Parmesan, chicken and
    anchovy salad 42
apple juice
  all the blues 26
  spinach and banana 28
apples
  baked apple and banana with
    oaty crumble top and
    bottom 182
  pork rissoles with apple and
    fennel purée 72
  sweet potato and apple soup
    24
aubergines
  imam bayildi 136
  Mediterranean roasted
    vegetable and feta bowl
    160
avocados
  beef and jalapeño burger with
    guacamole 80
  herbed chickpea and olive
    salad 54
  salmon and avocado rice
    bowl 162
  smoked mackerel, watercress
    and courgette salad with
    avocado horseradish
    dressing 52
  smoked salmon, avocado and
    wasabi stack 108–9

bananas
  baked apple and banana with
    oaty crumble top and
    bottom 182

breakfast smoothie bowl 144
  seedy banana peanut butter
    oat cookies 168
  spinach and banana 28
basa, river cobbler with broad
    bean mash and lime rocket
    salad 90
basil, green pasta 148
beans
  bangin' bean burger 124
  bean and beetroot salad with
    rocket and pesto 54
  black bean chilli 138
  classic Niçoise salad 40
  cod and chorizo one pot 110
  courgette, cannellini, coconut
    and tomato stew 120
  red lentil, white bean and
    butternut squash stew
    116
  river cobbler with broad bean
    mash and lime rocket
    salad 90
  roasted roots with creamy
    white bean purée 128
  salmon and avocado rice
    bowl 162
  tomato and white bean soup
    24
beef
  beef and beetroot casserole
    82
  beef, broccoli and ginger stir-
    fry 66
  beef and jalapeño burger with
    guacamole 80
  warm steak salad 60
beetroot
  all the blues 26

bean and beetroot salad with
    rocket and pesto 54
  beef and beetroot casserole
    82
  beetroot and horseradish
    soup 16
  cauliflower 'steak' with
    balsamic root roast 134
  roasted red onion, beetroot
    and goats' cheese salad
    34
  roasted roots with creamy
    white bean purée 128
berries
  all the blues 26
  breakfast smoothie bowl 144
broccoli, beef, broccoli and
    ginger stir-fry 66
butternut squash
  gingered squash soup 16
  red lentil, white bean and
    butternut squash stew
    116
  sausage, sage and squash
    one-tray roast 64

carrots
  all-in-one egg fried rice 154
  cauliflower 'steak' with
    balsamic root roast 134
  hummus, roasted onion and
    rainbow slaw wrap 130
  roasted carrot and
    cauliflower soup 22
  roasted roots with creamy
    white bean purée 128
  Thai-style veggie 'noodle'
    salad 50
  warm steak salad 60

cauliflower
  cauliflower 'steak' with
    balsamic root roast 134
  dreamy creamy cauliflower
    soup 22
  roasted carrot and
    cauliflower soup 22
cheese
  chicken with peppered
    mushroom sauce 62
  fig and feta salad 38
  goats' cheese and roasted
    vegetable salad 44
  kale, Parmesan, chicken and
    anchovy salad 42
  Mediterranean roasted
    vegetable and feta bowl
    160
  peach, blue cheese and
    watercress salad 48
  quinoa, pea, mint and feta
    salad with lime dressing
    46
  river cobbler with broad bean
    mash and lime rocket
    salad 90
  roasted red onion, beetroot
    and goats' cheese salad
    34
  turkey stuffed peppers 68
  veggie-packed penne with
    feta 152
chicken
  chicken with peppered
    mushroom sauce 62
  chicken with spring onions in
    satay sauce 74
  chicken tagliatelle with
    roasted red pepper sauce
    158
  Chinese roast chicken 70
  kale, Parmesan, chicken and
    anchovy salad 42
  ramen bowl 146
chickpeas

chocolate chickpea bars
  180
herbed chickpea and olive
  salad 54
hummus, roasted onion and
  rainbow slaw wrap 130
speedy chickpea and spinach
  curry 132
sweet potato and chickpea
  bake 118
chillies
  beef and jalapeño burger with
    guacamole 80
  chilli and lime salmon
    parcels 102
  chilli prawns with red onion
    and courgettes 100
  fancy fish curry 94
Chinese roast chicken 70
chocolate
  chocolate chickpea bars 182
  crunchy chocolate trail bark
    170
  raw brownies 174
chorizo, cod and chorizo one
  pot 110
coconut
  fridge bars 186
  ginger date balls 184
coconut milk
  courgette, cannellini, coconut
    and tomato stew 120
  dreamy creamy cauliflower
    soup 22
  fancy fish curry 94
  green curry noodles 150
  piña no lada 28
cod
  cod and chorizo one pot 110
  fancy fish curry 94
coriander
  bangin' bean burger 124
  chicken with spring onions in
    satay sauce 74
  green curry noodles 150

salmon burgers with chilli
  aioli 96
courgettes
  chilli prawns with red onion
    and courgettes 100
  courgette, cannellini, coconut
    and tomato stew 120
  fig and feta salad 38
  goats' cheese and roasted
    vegetable salad 44
  green curry noodles 150
  green pasta 148
  herbed turkey meatballs with
    courgette couscous 78
  Mediterranean roasted
    vegetable and feta bowl
    160
  smoked mackerel, watercress
    and courgette salad with
    avocado horseradish
    dressing 52
  sun-dried tomato, courgette
    and red pepper risotto
    126
  Thai-style veggie 'noodle'
    salad 50
  veggie-packed penne with
    feta 152
couscous, herbed turkey
  meatballs with courgette
  couscous 78

dates
  fridge bars 186
  ginger date balls 184
  raw brownies 174

eggs
  all-in-one egg fried
    rice 154
  classic Niçoise salad 40
  ramen bowl 146

fennel, pork rissoles with apple
  and fennel purée 72

figs
  baked figs with ginger
    yoghurt and seeds 176
  fig and feta salad 38
fridge bars 186

ginger
  baked figs with ginger
    yoghurt and seeds 176
  beef, broccoli and ginger stir-
    fry 66
  chilli and lime salmon
    parcels 102
  easy king prawn curry 104
  ginger date balls 184
  gingered squash soup 16

honey
  baked apple and banana with
    oaty crumble top and
    bottom 182
  beef and beetroot casserole
    82
  Chinese roast chicken 70
  fridge bars 186
  honey mustard pork chops
    with kale and mushroom
    sauté 76
  honey roasted cashews 178
  imam bayildi 136
  nutty noodles 122
  pears poached in spiced
    red wine 172
  seedy banana peanut butter
    oat cookies 168
horseradish
  beetroot and horseradish
    soup 16
  smoked mackerel, watercress
    and courgette salad with
    avocado horseradish
    dressing 52
hummus, roasted onion
    and rainbow slaw
    wrap 130

kale
  all-in-one egg fried rice 154
  the famous kale salad 36
  honey mustard pork chops
    with kale and mushroom
    sauté 76
  kale, Parmesan, chicken and
    anchovy salad 42
  pork rissoles with apple and
    fennel purée 72
  vibrant vichyssoise 18

leeks, vibrant vichyssoise 18
lemon grass, fancy fish curry
    94
lentils
  fancy fish curry 94
  red lentil, white bean and
    butternut squash stew
    116
lettuce, classic Niçoise salad
    40
limes
  beef and jalapeño burger with
    guacamole 80
  chilli and lime salmon
    parcels 102
  maple mustard salmon with
    paprika sweet potato
    wedges and green salad
    106
  Pad Thai upgraded 156
  quinoa, pea, mint and feta
    salad with lime dressing
    46
  river cobbler with broad bean
    mash and lime rocket
    salad 90
  Thai-style veggie 'noodle'
    salad 50

mango peach smoothie 26
maple syrup
  chocolate chickpea
    bars 180

maple mustard salmon
    with paprika sweet
    potato wedges and
    green salad 106
raw brownies 174
Mediterranean roasted
    vegetable and feta bowl 160
mint, quinoa, pea, mint and
    feta salad with lime
    dressing 46
miso paste, ramen bowl 146
mushrooms
  all-in-one egg fried rice 154
  chicken with peppered
    mushroom sauce 62
  goats' cheese and roasted
    vegetable salad 44
  green curry noodles 150
  honey mustard pork chops
    with kale and mushroom
    sauté 76
  Mediterranean roasted
    vegetable and feta bowl
    160
  nutty noodles 122
  ramen bowl 146
  three mushroom soup 20

noodles
  green curry noodles 150
  nutty noodles 122
  Pad Thai upgraded 156
  ramen bowl 146
nuts
  ginger date balls 184
  honey roasted cashews 178
  Pad Thai upgraded 156
  raw brownies 174
  Thai-style veggie 'noodle'
    salad 50

oats
  baked apple and banana
    with oaty crumble top
    and bottom 182

seedy banana peanut
butter oat cookies
168
olives
classic Niçoise salad 40
herbed chickpea and olive
salad 54
salmon, red pepper and
black olive stew 92

Pad Thai upgraded 156
paella, pimped-up 98
parsnips, roasted roots
with creamy white bean
purée 128
pasta
chicken tagliatelle with
roasted red pepper
sauce 158
green pasta 148
veggie-packed penne with
feta 152
peaches, mango peach 26
peanut butter
chicken with spring onions
in satay sauce 74
nutty noodles 122
seedy banana peanut butter
oat cookies 168
pears poached in spiced red
wine 172
peas
green pasta 148
pork rissoles with apple and
fennel purée 72
quinoa, pea, mint and
feta salad with lime
dressing 46
tuna and sweet potato
fish cakes 88
vibrant vichyssoise 18
peppers
chicken tagliatelle with
roasted red pepper
sauce 158

goats' cheese and roasted
vegetable salad 44
Mediterranean roasted
vegetable and feta
bowl 160
salmon, red pepper and
black olive stew 92
sun-dried tomato, courgette
and red pepper risotto
126
turkey stuffed peppers 68
pesto, bean and beetroot
salad with rocket and
pesto 54
pimped-up paella 98
pineapple, piña no lada 28
pork
honey mustard pork chops
with kale and mushroom
sauté 76
pork rissoles with apple and
fennel purée 72
potatoes
classic Niçoise salad 40
vibrant vichyssoise 18
prawns
chilli prawns with red onion
and courgettes 100
easy king prawn curry 104
green curry noodles 150
Pad Thai upgraded 156

quinoa, pea, mint and feta salad
with lime dressing 46

ramen bowl 146
red cabbage, hummus, roasted
onion and rainbow slaw
wrap 130
red onions
chilli prawns with red onion
and courgettes 100
fig and feta salad 38
goats' cheese and roasted
vegetable salad 44

herbed turkey meatballs with
courgette couscous 78
hummus, roasted onion and
rainbow slaw wrap 130
Mediterranean roasted
vegetable and feta
bowl 160
roasted red onion, beetroot
and goats' cheese
salad 34
roasted roots with creamy
white bean purée 128
salmon burgers with chilli
aioli 96
sausage, sage and squash
one-tray roast 64
veggie-packed penne with
feta 152
rice
all-in-one egg fried rice 154
pimped-up paella 98
sun-dried tomato, courgette
and red pepper risotto 126
river cobbler with broad bean
mash and lime rocket salad
90
rocket
river cobbler with broad bean
mash and lime rocket
salad 90
warm steak salad 60

sage
pork rissoles with apple and
fennel purée 72
sausage, sage and squash
one-tray roast 64
salmon
chilli and lime salmon
parcels 102
fancy fish curry 94
maple mustard salmon with
paprika sweet potato
wedges and green
salad 106

salmon and avocado rice bowl 162

salmon burgers with chilli aioli 96

salmon, red pepper and black olive stew 92

smoked salmon, avocado and wasabi stack 98

sausage, sage and squash one-tray roast 64

seafood, pimped-up paella 98

seeds

baked figs with ginger yoghurt and seeds 176

crunchy chocolate trail bark 170

fridge bars 186

seedy banana peanut butter oat cookies 168

smoked mackerel, watercress and courgette salad with avocado horseradish dressing 52

smoothies 26–28

breakfast smoothie bowl 144

spinach

courgette, cannellini, coconut and tomato stew 120

fancy fish curry 94

fig and feta salad 38

maple mustard salmon with paprika sweet potato wedges and green salad 106

Pad Thai upgraded 156

ramen bowl 146

salmon and avocado rice bowl 162

salmon burgers with chilli aioli 96

speedy chickpea and spinach curry 132

spinach and banana 28

sweet potato and chickpea bake 118

veggie-packed penne with feta 152

spring greens, cauliflower 'steak' with balsamic root roast 134

spring onions, chicken with spring onions in satay sauce 74

squid, green curry noodles 150

sugar snap peas, maple mustard salmon with paprika sweet potato wedges and green salad 106

sweet potatoes

maple mustard salmon with paprika sweet potato wedges and green salad 106

salmon, red pepper and black olive stew 92

sweet potato and apple soup 24

sweet potato and chickpea bake 118

tuna and sweet potato fish cakes 88

tahini

fridge bars 186

hummus, roasted onion and rainbow slaw wrap 130

roasted roots with creamy white bean purée 128

Thai-style veggie 'noodle' salad 50

tofu

all-in-one egg fried rice 154

nutty noodles 122

tomatoes

black bean chilli 138

classic Niçoise salad 40

cod and chorizo one pot 110

courgette, cannellini, coconut and tomato stew 120

easy king prawn curry 104

the famous kale salad 36

herbed chickpea and olive salad 54

herbed turkey meatballs with courgette couscous 78

imam bayildi 136

pimped-up paella 98

salmon, red pepper and black olive stew 92

speedy chickpea and spinach curry 132

sun-dried tomato, courgette and red pepper risotto 126

tomato and white bean soup 24

warm steak salad 60

tuna

classic Niçoise salad 40

tuna and sweet potato fish cakes 88

turkey

herbed turkey meatballs with courgette couscous 78

turkey stuffed peppers 68

vibrant vichyssoise 18

wasabi, smoked salmon, avocado and wasabi stack 108–9

watercress, smoked mackerel, watercress and courgette salad with avocado horseradish dressing 52

yoghurt

all the blues 26

baked figs with ginger yoghurt and seeds 176

easy king prawn curry 104

mango peach 26

peach, blue cheese and watercress salad 48

piña no lada 28

Newport Community
Learning & Libraries